Learning Material Design

Master Material Design and create beautiful, animated interfaces for mobile and web applications

Kyle Mew

BIRMINGHAM - MUMBAI

Learning Material Design

First published: December 2015

Production reference: 1181215

Published by Packt Publishing Ltd.
Livery Place
35 Livery Street
Birmingham B3 2PB, UK.

ISBN 978-1-78528-981-1

www.packtpub.com

Credits

Author
Kyle Mew

Reviewer
Will Haering

Commissioning Editor
Ashwin Nair

Acquisition Editors
Vivek Anantharaman

Harsha Bharwani

Content Development Editor
Priyanka Mehta

Technical Editor
Mohita Vyas

Copy Editor
Angad Singh

Project Coordinator
Izzat Contractor

Proofreader
Safis Editing

Indexer
Rekha Nair

Graphics
Abhinash Sahu

Production Coordinator
Melwyn D'sa

Cover Work
Melwyn D'sa

About the Author

Kyle Mew has been programming since the early eighties and has written for several technology websites. He has also written three radio plays and two other books on Android development.

I would like to dedicate this book to Amber and thank her for being a constant inspiration throughout.

About the Reviewer

Will Haering is a self-taught frontend developer, with significant experience in both web technologies and data processing. He has been designing and developing sites and web apps for 5 years, starting as a freelancer and then switching paths to begin working as a client engineer for Symphony Commerce in San Francisco. Earlier in 2015, he participated in a research project on studying the evidence of gravitational waves. He did this by processing NASA's test data using Julia. In 2014, as a member of the Precision Engineering Research Group at the Massachusetts Institute of Technology, Will developed an audio analysis script with industrial and agricultural applications. He is currently completing his senior year of high school at Phillips Exeter Academy. You can find him online at `http://www.wch.io/`.

www.PacktPub.com

Support files, eBooks, discount offers, and more

For support files and downloads related to your book, please visit www.PacktPub.com.

Did you know that Packt offers eBook versions of every book published, with PDF and ePub files available? You can upgrade to the eBook version at www.PacktPub.com and as a print book customer, you are entitled to a discount on the eBook copy. Get in touch with us at service@packtpub.com for more details.

At www.PacktPub.com, you can also read a collection of free technical articles, sign up for a range of free newsletters and receive exclusive discounts and offers on Packt books and eBooks.

https://www2.packtpub.com/books/subscription/packtlib

Do you need instant solutions to your IT questions? PacktLib is Packt's online digital book library. Here, you can search, access, and read Packt's entire library of books.

Why subscribe?

- Fully searchable across every book published by Packt
- Copy and paste, print, and bookmark content
- On demand and accessible via a web browser

Free access for Packt account holders

If you have an account with Packt at www.PacktPub.com, you can use this to access PacktLib today and view 9 entirely free books. Simply use your login credentials for immediate access.

Table of Contents

Preface

Welcome to *Learning Material Design*, a comprehensive guide to the latest and hottest design philosophy for mobile and web applications. More than just a design language, Material Design represents a powerful shift in how modern digital interfaces look and behave. Based largely on traditional design principles, Material Design brings a tactile look and feel to apps and pages, giving screen elements physical properties such as fluid, realistic motion and the ability to depict a third dimension using shadows.

Covering all major design principles and guidelines and including enough of the technologies and code required to implement them, the book is designed so that you can get started with building your own material interfaces from the very beginning.

All the commonly used material components, such as cards and sliding drawers, are covered in terms of both design guidelines and code structures. This element-specific approach is coupled with details on how Material Design can be applied to interfaces in general, and how to use these guidelines to create material transitions and navigation processes.

Although concentrating largely on mobile interface design and using the powerful Android Studio development environment, the latter part of the book focuses on how the principles learned earlier can be just as easily applied to designs of web and desktop interfaces with a number of helpful and simple-to-use CSS frameworks, particularly Materialize and Material Design Lite.

This book is only the beginning of a journey into what may well become one of the most persistent digital design paradigms we have yet seen. But by the end, you will have learned not only the design theory behind materials, but also enough of technical know-how to put what you have learned into practice and be in a position to create or convert Material Design applications on your own.

What this book covers

Chapter 1, Getting Started with Material Design, introduces some of the basic precepts of Material Design, but concentrates largely on how to set up a development environment and create a simple "Hello World" app. This includes an introduction to the material theme and palette.

Chapter 2, Building a Mobile Layout, is where we concentrate on some fundamental processes in designing an Android interface, such as the content hierarchy and how components are positioned and scaled within it. The second portion of this chapter covers support libraries and how these can help us make Material Design backward compatible.

Chapter 3, Common Components, covers the most frequently used mobile material components, such as app bars, menus, and modal dialogs, along with the creation of action icons for menus.

Chapter 4, Sliding Drawers and Navigation, explains the typical material navigation techniques, in particular, the navigation menu and sliding drawers.

Chapter 5, Lists, Cards, and Data, is where we see how the recycler view can be used to organize data in the form of a list, and how separate fields of mixed media can be applied to the card view widget.

Chapter 6, Animations and Transitions, covers transition from one screen to another, including hide and reveal animations and how components that are shared across screens are animated.

Chapter 7, Material on Other Devices, is where we look at how Material Design is applied to the Android TV and Wear platforms.

Chapter 8, Material Web Frameworks, takes us on a brief tour of one of the most commonly used technologies for applying Material Design to web pages. This is done using ready-made CSS and JavaScript frameworks.

Chapter 9, The Materialize Framework, delves deeper into the Materialize web frameworks, demonstrating how common components, animations, and navigation are achieved.

Chapter 10, Material Design Lite, is the final chapter. It covers the most popular material framework — Material Design Lite. As in the previous chapter, we explore the most commonly used components and features.

What you need for this book

Android Studio and SDK are both open source and free, and instructions on installation and configuration are included in the book.

Who this book is for

This book is ideal for web developers and designers who are interested in implementing Material Design in their mobile and web apps. No prior knowledge or experience of Material Design is required, but some familiarity with procedural languages such as Java and markup languages such as HTML will provide an advantage.

Conventions

In this book, you will find a number of text styles that distinguish between different kinds of information. Here are some examples of these styles and an explanation of their meaning.

Code words in text, database table names, folder names, filenames, file extensions, pathnames, dummy URLs, user input, and Twitter handles are shown as follows: "The Tools directory contains exactly what it says, that is, tools."

A block of code is set as follows:

```
<TextView
    android:id="@+id/text_view"
    android:layout_width="wrap_content"
    android:layout_height="wrap_content"
    android:layout_centerHorizontal="true"
    android:layout_centerVertical="true"
    android:text="@string/hello_world" />
```

When we wish to draw your attention to a particular part of a code block, the relevant lines or items are set in bold:

```
<TextView
    android:id="@+id/name"
    android:layout_width="wrap_content"
    android:layout_height="wrap_content"
    android:layout_alignParentTop="true"
    android:layout_toRightOf="@+id/profile_pic"
    android:textSize="24sp" />
```

Any command-line input or output is written as follows:

```
bower install <package>
bower update <package>
bower search <containing>
bower list
```

New terms and **important words** are shown in bold. Words that you see on the screen, for example, in menus or dialog boxes, appear in the text like this: "You can then open the SDK manager from the menu via **Tools** | **Android** | **SDK Manager** or the matching icon on the main toolbar."

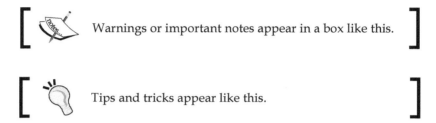

Warnings or important notes appear in a box like this.

Tips and tricks appear like this.

Reader feedback

Feedback from our readers is always welcome. Let us know what you think about this book—what you liked or disliked. Reader feedback is important for us as it helps us develop titles that you will really get the most out of.

To send us general feedback, simply e-mail feedback@packtpub.com, and mention the book's title in the subject of your message.

If there is a topic that you have expertise in and you are interested in either writing or contributing to a book, see our author guide at www.packtpub.com/authors.

Customer support

Now that you are the proud owner of a Packt book, we have a number of things to help you to get the most from your purchase.

Downloading the color images of this book

We also provide you with a PDF file that has color images of the screenshots/diagrams used in this book. The color images will help you better understand the changes in the output. You can download this file from https://www.packtpub.com/sites/default/files/downloads/LearningMaterialDesign_ColoredImages.pdf.

Errata

Although we have taken every care to ensure the accuracy of our content, mistakes do happen. If you find a mistake in one of our books—maybe a mistake in the text or the code—we would be grateful if you could report this to us. By doing so, you can save other readers from frustration and help us improve subsequent versions of this book. If you find any errata, please report them by visiting http://www.packtpub.com/submit-errata, selecting your book, clicking on the **Errata Submission Form** link, and entering the details of your errata. Once your errata are verified, your submission will be accepted and the errata will be uploaded to our website or added to any list of existing errata under the Errata section of that title.

To view the previously submitted errata, go to https://www.packtpub.com/books/content/support and enter the name of the book in the search field. The required information will appear under the **Errata** section.

Piracy

Piracy of copyrighted material on the Internet is an ongoing problem across all media. At Packt, we take the protection of our copyright and licenses very seriously. If you come across any illegal copies of our works in any form on the Internet, please provide us with the location address or website name immediately so that we can pursue a remedy.

Please contact us at copyright@packtpub.com with a link to the suspected pirated material.

We appreciate your help in protecting our authors and our ability to bring you valuable content.

Questions

If you have a problem with any aspect of this book, you can contact us at questions@packtpub.com, and we will do our best to address the problem.

1
Getting Started with Material Design

Google first announced Material Design at their I/O conference in the summer of 2014, and it has since gone on to create quite a storm among developers and designers alike. Originally a formalization and expansion of the Google Now UI, Material Design has grown (and is still growing) into a comprehensive and systematic set of design philosophies.

Material can be thought of as something like smart paper. Like paper, it has surfaces and edges that reflect light and cast shadows, but unlike paper, material has properties that real paper does not, such as its ability to move, change its shape and size, and merge with other material. Despite this seemingly magical behavior, material should be treated like a physical object with a physicality of its own.

Material can be seen as existing in a three-dimensional space, and it is this that gives its interfaces a reassuring sense of depth and structure. Hierarchies become obvious when it is instantly clear whether an object is above or below another.

Based largely on age-old principles taken from color theory, animation, traditional print design, and physics, Material Design provides a virtual space where developers can use surface and light to create meaningful interfaces and movement to design intuitive user interactions.

This book covers both the design principles and the tools required to create the elegant and responsive interfaces that have made Material Design so popular and successful. The journey begins with the Android SDK and Android Studio, which we will use to build working material UIs for a variety of form factors, ranging from tiny wearable devices to large flat screen TVs. This will provide a solid foundation for the design principles behind the subject, and how mobile interfaces are defined using XML and then brought to life with Java.

With the aspects of design covered, the book concludes by exploring the different guidelines and tools required to build material web apps. There are several subtle differences in the design rules, and the possible absence of a touch-screen on desktop computers requires a different approach to user interaction. More significantly, when building web pages, we will need to work in HTML, and to implement material, we will need a tool called **Polymer** and its associate, **Paper Elements**.

With the journey outlined, we will begin by taking a quick look at the physical properties of material, and then we'll dive straight in and produce our first interface. To do this, we will need to download and configure Android Studio and SDK tools, as well as create a device emulator to compile and run our apps on. With our development environment in place, we can then take a look at the material themes available as default on recent Android versions.

In this chapter, you will learn how to:

- Understand the physical properties of material
- Install Android Studio
- Configure the Android SDK
- Install Google support libraries
- Create a virtual device
- Set up a real device for development
- Create a hello world app in Android Studio
- Create an Android style with XML
- Customize the material theme
- Apply a material palette

Material properties

As mentioned in the introduction, material can be thought of as being bound by physical laws. There are things it can do and things it cannot. It can split apart and heal again, and change color and shape, but it cannot occupy the same space as another sheet of material or rotate around two of its axes. We will be dealing with these properties throughout the book, but it is a good idea to begin with a quick look at the things material can and can't do.

The third dimension is fundamental when it comes to material. This is what gives the user the illusion that they are interacting with something more tangible than a rectangle of light. The illusion is generated by the widening and softening of shadows beneath material that is *closer* to the user. Material exists in virtual space, but a space that, nevertheless, represents the real dimensions of a phone or tablet. The *x* axis can be thought of as existing between the top and bottom of the screen, the *y* axis between the right and left edges, and the *z* axis confined to the space between the back of the handset and the glass of the screen. It is for this reason that material should not rotate around the *x* or *y* axes, as this would break the illusion of a space inside the phone.

The basic laws of the physics of material are outlined, as follows, in the form of a list:

- All material is 1 dp thick (along the *z* axis).
- Material is solid, only one sheet can exist in one place at a time and material cannot pass through other material. For example, if a card needs to move past another, it must move over it.
- Elevation, or position along the *z* axis, is portrayed by shadow, with higher objects having wider, softer shadows.
- The *z* axis should be used to prompt interaction. For example, an action button rising up toward the user to demonstrate that it can be used to perform some action.
- Material does not fold or bend.
- Material cannot appear to rise higher than the screen surface.
- Material can grow and shrink along both *x* and *y* axes.
- Material can move along any axis.
- Material can be spontaneously created and destroyed, but this must not be without movement. The arrivals and departures of material components must be animated. For example, a card growing from the point that it was summoned from or sliding off the screen when dismissed.
- A sheet of material can split apart anywhere along the *x* or *y* axes, and join together again with its original partner or with other material.

This covers the basic rules of material behavior but we have said nothing of its content. If material can be thought of as smart paper, then its content can only be described as smart ink. The rules governing how ink behaves are a little simpler:

- Material content can be text, imagery, or any other form of visual digital content

- Content can be of any shape or color and behaves independently from its container material

- It cannot be displayed beyond the edges of its material container

- It adds nothing to the thickness (z axis) of the material it is displayed on

Setting up a development environment

The Android development environment consists mainly of two distinct components: the SDK, which provides the code libraries behind Android and Android Studio, and a powerful code editor that is used for constructing and testing applications for Android phones and tablets, Wear, TV, Auto, Glass, and Cardboard. Both these components can both be downloaded as a single package from `http://developer.android.com/sdk/index.html`.

Installing Android Studio

The installation is very straightforward. Run the Android Studio bundle and follow the on-screen instructions, installing **HAXM** hardware acceleration if prompted, and selecting all SDK components, as shown here:

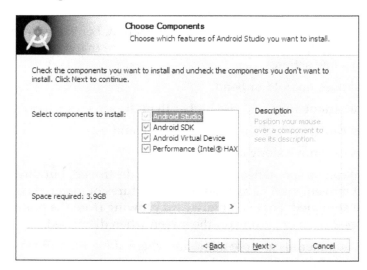

Android Studio is dependent on the **Java JDK**. If you have not previously installed it, this will be detected while you are installing Android Studio, and you will be prompted to download and install it. If for some reason it does not, it can be found at `http://www.oracle.com/technetwork/java/javase/downloads/index.html`, from where you should download the latest version.

This is not quite the end of the installation process. There are still some SDK components that we will need to download manually before we can build our first app. As we will see next, this is done using the **Android SDK Manager**.

Configuring the Android SDK

People often refer to Android versions by name, such as Lollipop, or an identity number, such as 5.1.1. As developers, it makes more sense to use the API level, which in the case of Android 5.1.1 would be API level 22. The SDK provides a platform for every API level since API level 8 (Android 2.2). In this section, we will use the SDK Manager to take a closer look at Android platforms, along with the other tools included in the SDK.

Start a new Android Studio project or open an existing one with the minimum SDK at 21 or higher. You can then open the SDK manager from the menu via **Tools | Android | SDK Manager** or the matching icon on the main toolbar.

 The Android SDK Manager can also be started as a stand alone program. It can be found in the `/Android/sdk` directory, as can the **Android Virtual Device (AVD)** manager.

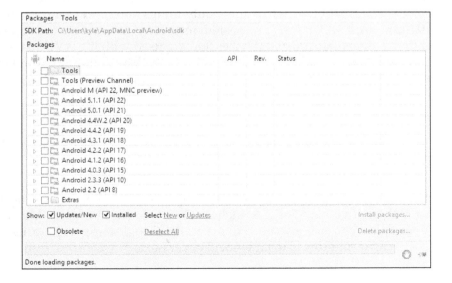

As can be seen in the preceding screenshot, there are really three main sections in the SDK:

- A `Tools` folder
- A collection of platforms
- An `Extras` folder

All these require a closer look. The `Tools` directory contains exactly what it says, that is, tools. There are a handful of these but the ones that will concern us are the SDK manager that we are using now, and the AVD manager that we will be using shortly to create a virtual device.

Open the `Tools` folder. You should find the latest revisions of the SDK tools and the SDK Platform-tools already installed. If not, select these items, along with the latest Build-tools, that is, if they too have not been installed.

 These tools are often revised, and it is well worth it to regularly check the SDK manager for updates.

When it comes to the platforms themselves, it is usually enough to simply install the latest one. This does not mean that these apps will not work on or be available to devices running older versions, as we can set a minimum SDK level when setting up a project, and along with the use of support libraries, we can bring Material Design to almost any Android device out there.

If you open up the folder for the latest platform, you will see that some items have already been installed. Strictly speaking, the only things you need to install are the SDK platform itself and at least one system image. System images are copies of the hard drives of actual Android devices and are used with the AVD to create emulators. Which images you use will depend on your system and the form factors that you are developing for. In this book, we will be building apps for phones and tablets, so make sure you use one of these at least.

 Although they are not required to develop apps, the documentation and samples packages can be extremely useful.

At the bottom of each platform folder are the Google APIs and corresponding system images. Install these if you are going to include Google services, such as Maps and Cloud, in your apps. You will also need to install the Google support libraries from the `Extras` directory, and this is what we will cover next.

The Extras folder contains various miscellaneous packages with a range of functions. The ones you are most likely to want to download are listed as follows:

- Android support libraries are invaluable extensions to the SDK that provide APIs that not only facilitate backwards compatibility, but also provide a lot of extra components and functions, and most importantly for us, the design library. As we are developing on Android Studio, we need only install the **Android Support Repository**, as this contains the **Android Support Library** and is designed for use with Android.

- The **Google Play** services and **Google Repository** packages are required, along with the Google APIs mentioned a moment ago, to incorporate Google Services into an application.

- You will most likely need the **Google USB Driver** if you are intending to test your apps on a real device. How to do this will be explained later in this chapter.

- The HAXM installer is invaluable if you have a recent Intel processor. Android emulators can be notoriously slow, and this hardware acceleration can make a noticeable difference.

Once you have downloaded your selected SDK components, depending on your system and/or project plans, you should have a list of installed packages similar to the one shown next:

Name	API	Rev.	Status
Tools			
Android SDK Tools		24.3.3	Installed
Android SDK Platform-tools		22	Installed
Android SDK Build-tools		22.0.1	Installed
Android 5.1.1 (API 22)			
Documentation for Android SDK	22	1	Installed
SDK Platform	22	2	Installed
Samples for SDK	22	6	Installed
Intel x86 Atom_64 System Image	22	1	Installed
Google APIs	22	1	Installed
Google APIs Intel x86 Atom System Image	22	1	Installed
Extras			
Android Support Repository		15	Installed
Google Play services		25	Installed
Google Repository		19	Installed
Google USB Driver		11	Installed
Intel x86 Emulator Accelerator (HAXM installer)		5.3	Installed

The SDK is finally ready, and we can start developing material interfaces. All that is required now is a device to test it on. This can, of course, be done on an actual device, but generally speaking, we will need to test our apps on as many devices as possible. Being able to emulate Android devices allows us to do this.

Emulating Android devices

The AVD allows us to test our designs across the entire range of form factors. There are an enormous number of screen sizes, shapes, and densities around. It is vital that we get to test our apps on as many device configurations as possible. This is actually more important for design than it is for functionality. An app might operate perfectly well on an exceptionally small or narrow screen, but not look as good as we had wanted, making the AVD one of the most useful tools available to us. This section covers how to create a virtual device using the AVD Manager.

The AVD Manager can be opened from within Android Studio by navigating to **Tools | Android | AVD Manager** from the menu or the corresponding icon on the toolbar. Here, you should click on the **Create Virtual Device...** button.

The easiest way to create an emulator is to simply pick a device definition from the list of hardware images and keep clicking on **Next** until you reach **Finish**. However, it is much more fun and instructive to either clone and edit an existing profile, or create one from scratch.

Click on the **New Hardware Profile** button. This takes you to the **Configure Hardware Profile** window where you will be able to create a virtual device from scratch, configuring everything from cameras and sensors, to storage and screen resolution. When you are done, click on **Finish** and you will be returned to the hardware selection screen where your new device will have been added:

Name	Size	Resolution	Density
Nexus S	4.0"	480x800	hdpi
Nexus One	3.7"	480x800	hdpi
Nexus 6	5.96"	1440x2560	560dpi
Nexus 5	4.95"	1080x1920	xxhdpi
Nexus 4	4.7"	768x1280	xhdpi
Material Device	5.0"	480x854	tvdpi
Galaxy Nexus	4.65"	720x1280	xhdpi
5.4" FWVGA	5.4"	480x854	mdpi
5.1" WVGA	5.1"	480x800	mdpi

As you will have seen from the **Import Hardware Profiles** button, it is possible to download system images for many devices not included with the SDK. Check the developer sections of device vendor's web sites to see which models are available.

So far, we have only configured the hardware for our virtual device. We must now select all the software it will use. To do this, select the hardware profile you just created and press **Next**. In the following window, select one of the system images you installed earlier and press **Next** again. This takes us to the **Verify Configuration** screen where the emulator can be fine-tuned. Most of these configurations can be safely left as they are, but you will certainly need to play with the scale when developing for high density devices. It can also be very useful to be able to use a real SD card. Once you click on **Finish**, the emulator will be ready to run.

 An emulator can be rotated through 90 degrees with left *Ctrl* + *F12*. The menu can be called with *F2*, and the back button with *ESC*. Keyboard commands to emulate most physical buttons, such as call, power, and volume, and a complete list can be found at http://developer.android.com/tools/help/emulator.html.

Android emulators are notoriously slow, during both loading and operating, even on quite powerful machines. The Intel hardware accelerator we encountered earlier can make a significant difference. Between the two choices offered, the one that you use should depend on how often you need to open and close a particular emulator. More often than not, taking advantage of your GPU is the more helpful of the two. Apart from this built-in assistance, there are a few other things you can do to improve performance, such as setting lower pixel densities, increasing the device's memory, and building the website for lower API levels. If you are comfortable doing so, set up exclusions in your anti-virus software for the Android Studio and SDK directories.

 There are several third-party emulators, such as Genymotion, that are not only faster, but also behave more like real devices.

The slowness of Android emulators is not necessarily a big problem, as most early development needs only one device, and real devices suffer none of the performance issues found on emulators. As we shall see next, real devices can be connected to our development environment with very little effort.

Connecting a real device

Using an actual physical device to run and test applications does not have the flexibility that emulators provide, but it does have one or two advantages of its own. Real devices are faster than any emulator, and you can test features unavailable to a virtual device, such as accessing sensors, and making and receiving calls.

There are two steps involved in setting up a real phone or tablet. We need to set developer options on the handset and configure the USB connection with our development computer:

1. To enable developer options on your handset, navigate to **Settings | About phone**. Tap on **Build number** 7 times to enable **Developer** options, which will now be available from the previous screen.

2. Open this to enable **USB debugging** and **Allow mock locations**.

3. Connect the device to your computer and check that it is connected as a **Media device (MTP)**.

Your handset can now be used as a test device. Depending on your We need only install the Google USB. Connect the device to your computer with a USB cable, start Android Studio, and open a project. Depending on your setup, it is quite possible that you are already connected. If not, you can install the Google USB driver by following these steps:

1. From the Windows start menu, open the device manager.

2. Your handset can be found under **Other Devices** or **Portable Devices**. Open its **Properties** window and select the **Driver** tab.

3. Update the driver with the Google version, which can be found in the `sdk\extras\google\usb_driver` directory.

An application can be compiled and run from Android Studio by selecting **Run 'app'** from the **Run** menu, pressing *Shift + F10*, or clicking on the green play icon on the toolbar. Once the project has finished building, you will be asked to confirm your choice of device before the app loads and then opens on your handset.

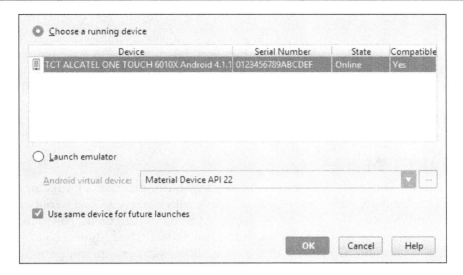

With a fully set up development environment and devices to test on, we can now start taking a look at Material Design, beginning with the material theme that is included as the default in all SDKs with APIs higher than 21.

The material theme

Since API level 21 (Android 5.0), the material theme has been the built-in user interface. It can be utilized and customized, simplifying the building of material interfaces. However, it is more than just a new look; the material theme also provides the automatic touch feedback and transition animations that we associate with Material Design.

To better understand Android themes and how to apply them, we need to understand how Android styles work, and a little about how screen components, such as buttons and text boxes, are defined.

Most individual screen components are referred to as widgets or views. Views that contain other views are called view groups, and they generally take the form of a layout, such as the relative layout we will use in a moment.

An **Android style** is a set of graphical properties defining the appearance of a particular screen component. Styles allow us to define everything from font size and background color, to padding elevation, and much more. An Android theme is simply a style applied across a whole screen or application. The best way to understand how this works is to put it into action and apply a style to a working project. This will also provide a great opportunity to become more familiar with Android Studio.

Applying styles

Styles are defined as XML files and are stored in the resources (`res`) directory of Android Studio projects. So that we can apply different styles to a variety of platforms and devices, they are kept separate from the layout code. To see how this is done, start a new project, selecting a minimum SDK of 21 or higher, and using the blank activity template. To the left of the editor is the project explorer pane. This is your access point to every branch of your project.

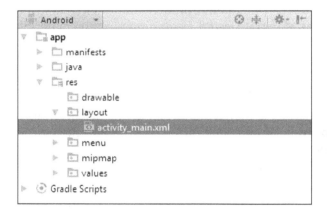

Take a look at the `activity_main.xml` file, which would have been opened in the editor pane when the project was created. At the bottom of the pane, you will see a **Text** tab and a **Design** tab. It should be quite clear, from examining these, how the XML code defines a text box (`TextView`) nested inside a window (`RelativeLayout`). Layouts can be created in two ways: textually and graphically. Usually, they are built using a combination of both techniques. In the design view, widgets can be dragged and dropped to form layout designs. Any changes made using the graphical interface are immediately reflected in the code, and experimenting with this is a fantastic way to learn how various widgets and layouts are put together. We will return to both these subjects in detail later on in the book, but for now, we will continue with styles and themes by defining a custom style for the text view in our Hello world app.

Open the `res` node in the project explorer; you can then right-click on the values node and select the **New | Values** resource file from the menu. Call this file `my_style` and fill it out as follows:

```xml
<?xml version="1.0" encoding="utf-8"?>
<resources>
    <style name="myStyle">
        <item name="android:layout_width">match_parent</item>
        <item name="android:layout_height">wrap_content</item>
        <item name="android:elevation">4dp</item>
        <item name="android:gravity">center_horizontal</item>
        <item name="android:padding">8dp</item>
        <item name="android:background">#e6e6e6</item>
        <item name="android:textSize">32sp</item>
        <item name="android:textColor">#727272</item>
    </style>
</resources>
```

This style defines several graphical properties, most of which should be self-explanatory with the possible exception of `gravity`, which here refers to how content is justified within the view. We will cover measurements and units later in the book, but for now, it is useful to understand **dp** and **sp**:

- **Density-independent pixel (dp)**: Android runs on an enormous number of devices, with screen densities ranging from 120 dpi to 480 dpi and more. To simplify the process of developing for such a wide variety, Android uses a virtual pixel unit based on a 160 dpi screen. This allows us to develop for a particular screen size without having to worry about screen density.

- **Scale-independent pixel (sp)**: This unit is designed to be applied to text. The reason it is scale-independent is because the actual text size on a user's device will depend on their font size settings.

To apply the style we just defined, open the `activity_main.xml` file (from `res/layouts`, if you have closed it) and edit the `TextView` node so that it matches this:

```xml
<TextView
    style="@style/myStyle"
    android:text="@string/hello_world" />
```

The effects of applying this style can be seen immediately from the design tab or preview pane, and having seen how styles are applied, we can now go ahead and create a style to customize the material theme palette.

Customizing the material theme

One of the most useful features of the material theme is the way it can take a small palette made of only a handful of colors and incorporate these colors into every aspect of a UI. Text and cursor colors, the way things are highlighted, and even system features such as the status and navigation bars can be customized to give our apps brand colors and an easily recognizable look.

The use of color in Material Design is a topic in itself, and there are strict guidelines regarding color, shade, and text, and these will be covered in detail later in the book. For now, we will just look at how we can use a style to apply our own colors to a material theme.

So as to keep our resources separate, and therefore easier to manage, we will define our palette in its own XML file. As we did earlier with the `my_style.xml` file, create a new values resource file in the `values` directory and call it `colors`. Complete the code as shown next:

```xml
<?xml version="1.0" encoding="utf-8"?>
<resources>
    <color name="primary">#FFC107</color>
    <color name="primary_dark">#FFA000</color>
    <color name="primary_light">#FFECB3</color>
    <color name="accent">#03A9F4</color>
    <color name="text_primary">#212121</color>
    <color name="text_secondary">#727272</color>
    <color name="icons">#212121</color>
    <color name="divider">#B6B6B6</color>
</resources>
```

In the gutter to the left of the code, you will see small, colored squares. Clicking on these will take you to a dialog with a color wheel and other color selection tools for quick color editing.

We are going to apply our style to the entire app, so rather than creating a separate file, we will include our style in the theme that was set up by the project template wizard when we started the project. This theme is called `AppTheme`, as can be seen by opening the `res/values/styles/styles.xml` (v21) file. Edit the code in this file so that it looks like the following:

```xml
<?xml version="1.0" encoding="utf-8"?>
<resources>
    <style name="AppTheme" parent="android:Theme.Material.Light">
        <item name="android:colorPrimary">@color/primary</item>
        <item name="android:colorPrimaryDark">@color/primary_dark</item>
        <item name="android:colorAccent">@color/accent</item>
        <item name="android:textColorPrimary">@color/text_primary</item>
        <item name="android:textColor">@color/text_secondary</item>
    </style>
</resources>
```

Being able to set key colors, such as `colorPrimary` and `colorAccent`, allows us to incorporate our brand colors throughout the app, although the project template only shows us how we have changed the color of the status bar and app bar. Try adding radio buttons or text edit boxes to see how the accent color is applied. In the following figure, a timepicker replaces the original text view:

The XML for this looks like the following lines:

```xml
<TimePicker
    android:layout_width="wrap_content"
    android:layout_height="wrap_content"
    android:layout_alignParentBottom="true"
    android:layout_centerHorizontal="true" />
```

For now, it is not necessary to know all the color guidelines. Until we get to them, there is an online material color palette generator at `http://www.materialpalette.com/` that lets you try out different palette combinations and download color XML files that can just be cut and pasted into the editor.

With a complete and up-to-date development environment constructed, and a way to customize and adapt the material theme, we are now ready to look into how material specific widgets, such as card views, are implemented.

Summary

The Android SDK, Android Studio, and AVD comprise a sophisticated development toolkit, and even setting them up is no simple task. But, with our tools in place, we were able to take a first look at one of Material Design's major components: the material theme. We have seen how themes and styles relate, and how to create and edit styles in XML. Finally, we have touched on material palettes, and how to customize a theme to utilize our own brand colors across an app.

With these basics covered, we can move on to explore Material Design further, and in the next chapter, we will look at layouts and material components in greater detail.

2
Building a Mobile Layout

Having set up Android Studio and SDK, along with real and virtual devices for testing on, and having had a brief look at one of the application templates provided by Android Studio, we are now in a position to take a more detailed look at how Android layouts are constructed, and how support libraries are used to create material layouts for older versions of Android.

There are several built-in layout formats provided with the SDK, and more available from the support libraries. As these layouts can be nested within one another, it is possible to put together almost any imaginable screen structure. This chapter will outline how screen components can be scaled, proportioned, and aligned, as well as how resources such as images and text are kept separate from layout definitions, and how this simplifies such things as translation. Although the content of this chapter is essential for creating material layouts, it does largely apply to all Android layouts in general.

After seeing how alternative layouts can be automatically generated to manage screen rotation, the latter part of the chapter concentrates on making Material Design available on older platforms, and how the new toolbar widget can be deployed in place of the older action bar.

In this chapter, we will cover the following topics:

- Create linear and relative layouts
- Combine ViewGroups to construct complex layouts
- Size widgets using weight properties
- Align content with gravity
- Scale images
- Translate text
- Generate layouts for managing screen rotation

- Use the `AppCompat` support library
- Apply the material theme to older versions
- Replace the old Action Bar with the material toolbar
- Apply material action icons

Activities and layouts

Android applications are are made up of one or more screens called activities. So as to keep design and function separate, the appearance of an activity is defined in XML, and its behavior with Java. Creating an Android Studio project using the **Blank Activity** template is a good way to see how this works.

XML activities contain two types of screen components. There are all the visible screen objects, called widgets, that we associate with mobile apps, such as buttons, sliders, and images, and there are invisible container objects known as layouts or ViewGroups. If you open the `activity_main.xml` XML file that was created by the project template, in design mode, you will see that there are seven layouts available to us at the top of the palette.

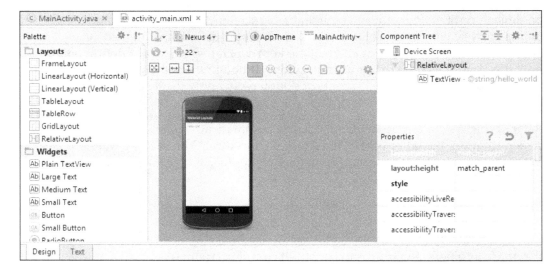

RelativeLayouts

On the right-hand side of the editor is the component tree; this displays a hierarchical view of the activity, and we can see that the root layout here is a RelativeLayout, and that it contains a single widget, TextView. RelativeLayout is an often used layout and is very useful because, as its name suggests, it allows us to position widgets and even other layouts relative to each other. This is particularly useful when it comes to the way a layout manages screen rotation, and it can also save memory as many complex layouts can be achieved without having to nest ViewGroups inside each other.

To see how relative layouts work, open the XML activity in graphical mode and drag the TextView to the center of the screen. Now, open the activity in text mode and add an android:id attribute to TextView, as seen here:

```
<TextView
    android:id="@+id/text_view"
    android:layout_width="wrap_content"
    android:layout_height="wrap_content"
    android:layout_centerHorizontal="true"
    android:layout_centerVertical="true"
    android:text="@string/hello_world" />
```

Once the view has a way of being referred to, other objects can be positioned and aligned in relation to it and each other if they too have IDs. Return to design mode and drag and drop some of the widgets or other views onto various parts of the design screen. This feature of the editor proves a very useful learning tool and allows us to write and understand code that is written automatically as we add and move screen components.

As you move items around the screen, a tip will appear at the top, outlining the attributes that are being applied.

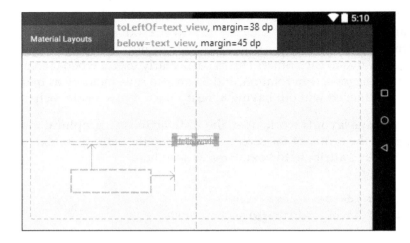

By experimenting a little with this, and examining the code after each change, one can become proficient very quickly in designing activities using a RelativeLayout.

LinearLayouts

The other most frequently used Android layout is LinearLayout. This layout is designed for single-column or single-row layouts, such as a list. Every linear layout has an `android:orientation` attribute that can take the values, horizontal or vertical. More complex designs can be achieved with LinearLayouts by nesting horizontal layouts inside vertical ones and vice versa, as can be seen in this layout:

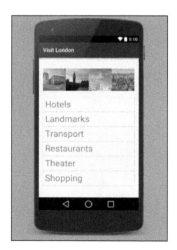

The preceding activity is constructed from three linear layouts, with a horizontal layout for the images nested alongside a vertical one for the text, inside a horizontal root layout. This can be seen more clearly by examining the component tree hierarchy:

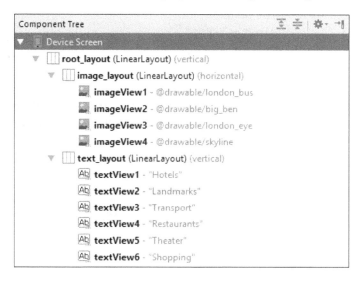

LinearLayout is a very convenient layout. It might seem that a single row or column might limit us as designers and developers, but by nesting them inside each other, we can create sophisticated and complex layouts. One thing that must be noted about LinearLayouts is that they consume a lot of resources; nesting too many can reduce performance and should only be done when the required result cannot be achieved using a RelativeLayout.

 Layouts and widgets can be re-positioned with the mouse from within the component tree.

Another very useful feature of LinearLayout is that relative weights can be assigned to individual widgets or groups. Widgets with an `android:layout_weight` attribute will share the space accordingly. This is best explained by example.

The following is the XML for one of the images in the previous layout:

```
<ImageView
    android:id="@+id/imageView1"
    android:layout_width="0dp"
    android:layout_height="128dp"
    android:layout_weight="1"
    android:src="@drawable/london_bus" />
```

The code is the same for all four ImageViews with the exception of their IDs and the `android:src` attribute, which points to the individual image resource. Importantly, they all have the same `layout_weight`. If we were to change the weights to 1, 2, 2, and 3 respectively, it would have the following result:

It is worth noting that the `layout_width` property is set to 0dp; this is because the property is compulsory, and setting it to other values interferes with the `weight` attribute.

RelativeLayouts and LinearLayouts are flexible enough to suit most purposes. There are several others that we will encounter: in particular, CoordinatorLayout and TabLayout, which are part of the design support library and created specifically for Material Design.

We have seen how Android Studio provides a graphical and textual interface for our layouts, and how the order and hierarchy can be easily edited with the component tree. There is one other useful way to view and edit an activity and that is the **Properties** pane, which we will use next to edit justification, or gravity, as it is referred to here.

Gravity properties

Just beneath **Component Tree** is the **Properties** pane. This provides a very simple way to add and edit the properties of our layouts and views, often providing drop-down lists to select from.

The gravity and layout_gravity properties control how the content of a view is justified within that view, and how the view is justified within its parent layout, respectively. To see the effects of content gravity, create TextView with its height and width both set to match_parent, and then use the **Properties** pane to change the gravity settings. As you can see in the next screenshot, there are over a dozen values that can be combined in a wide variety of ways:

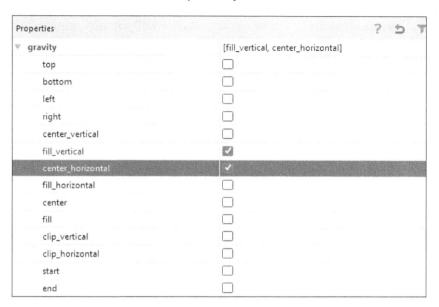

We have seen, thus far, in this chapter how to position and distribute a variety of widgets and view groups to form the visual aspect of an Android activity using built-in components. Often, of course, we will want to include graphics of our own, such as photographs and other images. As we shall see next, these can be easily added to the project and included in a layout.

Inserting and scaling images

We saw in the previous chapter that by using **density-independent pixels (dips)**, we can create layouts for devices of different sizes and resolutions with great ease. When it comes to including imagery, however, a little more consideration is required.

There is no difficulty in simply setting the width and height of an ImageView using the dp unit, but there are times when we risk losing image quality on very -high-density devices, and we need some way to calculate what size our original pictures need to be. The Android system assumes that a target device will have a density of 160 dpi (dots per inch); this means that on such a screen, a 100 x 100 pixel image will take up precisely that much space. But on a 640 dpi screen, the same area would cover 400 x 400 pixels, and we need to take this into consideration when producing our original images to avoid a loss of quality. As we will see in a minute, Android Studio allows us to very easily create alternative layouts for different screen sizes, but first, we need to see how to actually add images to our projects. Wide selections of screen densities can be tested directly from the graphical layout editor using the virtual device menu on the toolbar, as shown next:

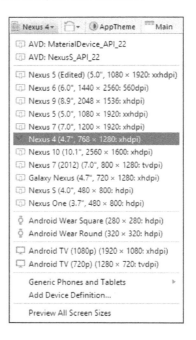

Images are stored as a resource in the `res/drawable` directory. This can be viewed using your system's file explorer from its sub-menu in the project explorer. Our chosen images can then simply be pasted into this folder and will then appear in the project explorer. Any format can be used, but PNGs are preferable and can be loaded into any view such as an ImageView with the `src` property, without spaces and excluding the file extension, as shown here:

```
android:src="@drawable/some_image"
```

This method of keeping resources and code separate is common throughout Android projects, and applies to a number of elements that we might not expect, such as string resources.

Strings and translation

When allocating some text to a view, such as `TextView`, it might seem logical to set it with something like the following lines:

```
<TextView
. . .
android:text="Some Text"
/>
```

Although this works perfectly well, it is highly discouraged as it muddles content with structure and makes translation virtually impossible.

Open the `strings.xml` file in the `res/values` folder. You will see something like this:

```
<resources>
    <string name="app_name">Some App</string>
    <string name="hello_world">Hello world!</string>
    <string name="action_settings">Settings</string>
    <string name="some_text">Some Text</string>
</resources>
```

All the strings used in our layouts should be defined in this resource file, although it is not necessary to edit the file directly, as the layout editor provides a very handy shortcut to define string resources:

1. Create or open `TextView` and provide a hardcoded string literal `android:text` value.

2. Place the cursor anywhere on the line and an amber quick fix icon will appear.

3. Select this and then the `Extract string resource` key from the drop-down, and you will be able to create the resource from a simple dialog:

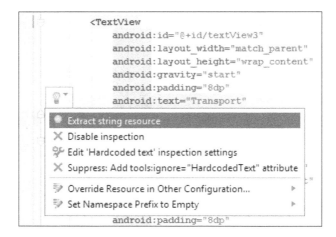

The real beauty of keeping string resources apart is that it makes producing translations of our apps very simple indeed. The translations editor can be opened from the `strings.xml` file's menu in the project explorer. Simply select the languages you want to translate into from the **Add Locale** icon at the top, and enter the translations in the fields at the bottom. This generates a new `strings.xml` file for each language you select, and any Android device running your app will automatically access these files in the appropriate locations.

Screen rotation

Many Android devices come with sensors that detect the orientation of the screen. When a device is rotated into landscape mode, the system redraws the layout according to the XML definition that we designed for portrait. Often, this is sufficient, but there are many times when a layout does not visually suit this orientation or make good use of the space. Fortunately, Android makes the process of managing this remarkably simple.

Take the following example of a simple relative layout:

Some layout configurations, although certainly not all, do not use up space well, or simply do not look nice in landscape mode. This can be mitigated to a degree through the judicious use of gravity and weight, but a far simpler and more elegant solution is to create an alternative layout file for landscape viewing. This takes only moments.

The layout configuration menu can be accessed from design mode by clicking on the leftmost icon and selecting **Create Landscape Variation**. You can now rearrange your views and view groups to better suit the screen proportions. Providing you leave other settings such as android:id the same, this new configuration will be automatically loaded every time a device is rotated into landscape mode.

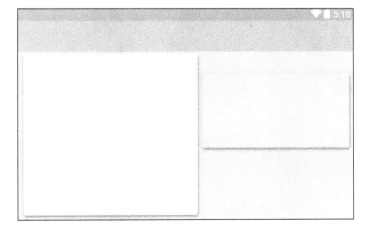

Checking the project explorer, you will see that the `res/layout/activity_main.xml` node now contains two files, our new configuration being called `activity_main.xml (land)`. If you look in the appropriate folder in your `AndroidStudioProjects` directory, you will see that it is, in fact, in a separate folder inside `app/src/main/res` called layout-land.

The configuration menu also allows us how to create layouts for large screens, along with a host of other useful preview and testing tools.

The material covered in this chapter applies to constructing Android layouts in general, and is not specific to Material Design. Most of the components and features that make up material UIs were introduced in API 21, and the way we implement them depends on whether we are developing for devices running Android 5.0 or higher, or if we hope to reach a wider audience by applying material to older versions. Very different approaches are required, depending on the choice we make here, as each option utilizes different code libraries and objects. There are a few disadvantages to making material backwards compatible, such as the loss of dynamic shadows and cards with rounded corners, but this is significantly outweighed by the increased number of potential users. There are also a number of workarounds we can use so that users running platform 5.0 or higher will experience all the material features, and only users of older handsets will get the paired down version. This can be achieved by creating alternative layouts, resources, and even Java code. All of this will be covered as we progress, but first we need to take that decision and see how material is applied on devices running platforms older than 5.0.

To help decide which platforms to target, Google has a very useful dashboard feature with relatively up-to-date device usage data:

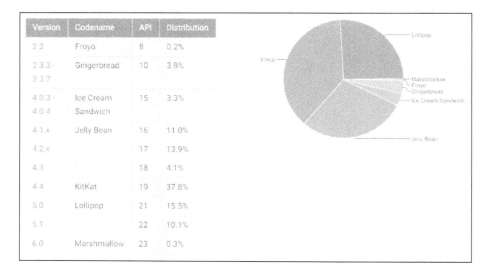

Version	Codename	API	Distribution
2.2	Froyo	8	0.2%
2.3.3 - 2.3.7	Gingerbread	10	3.8%
4.0.3 - 4.0.4	Ice Cream Sandwich	15	3.3%
4.1.x	Jelly Bean	16	11.0%
4.2.x		17	13.9%
4.3		18	4.1%
4.4	KitKat	19	37.8%
5.0	Lollipop	21	15.5%
5.1		22	10.1%
6.0	Marshmallow	23	0.3%

Applying material to older devices

The support repository we downloaded in the last chapter provides code that allows us to apply our designs on handsets going all the way back to Android 1.8, although the further back you go, the fewer features are supported. For the purpose of this book, we will make our applications backwards compatible as far back as API 16.

To achieve this, we will be using code provided by the AppCompat support library; in doing so, we will encounter one of the most significant material components: the Toolbar, which replaced the previous, less flexible Action Bar.

In older versions of Android, unless switched off, the Action Bar would sit at the top of each app and could contain our title along with any of the option menu items we chose, which were expressed as text, icons, or both. It was not really considered a true part of the UI, but rather an element that sat outside our design.

The new toolbar, although often acting as our app's action bar, is far more flexible and behaves like any other view within our own UI hierarchy. It can be placed anywhere, and can contain any elements we choose. Our layouts can even contain more than one.

The AppCompat support library

If you start a new project and select the **Minimum SDK** option to be lower than 21, the AppCompat library will be imported by default. Nevertheless, it is important to know how to do this so that we can convert existing projects created for 21 or higher, as well as for importing other support libraries. Open the build.gradle (Module: app) file from the project explorer. Support libraries should be added to the dependencies section, and the Appcompat library is the very minimum requirement for backwards compatibility:

```
dependencies {
    compile fileTree(dir: 'libs', include: ['*.jar'])
    compile 'com.android.support:appcompat-v7:23.1.1'
}
```

To explain the numbers, v7 refers to the minimum API level that the library caters to, and 23.1.1 references the latest revision. To find this, open the SDK manager and look in the **Rev.** column for the extras/Android Support Library files.

If you have not created the project for an older minimum SDK, you will need to edit the default configuration code to match the following:

```
defaultConfig {
    applicationId "com.mew.kyle.learningmaterialdesign"
    minSdkVersion 16
    targetSdkVersion 23
    versionCode 1
    versionName "1.0"
}
```

This library alone is not enough to make our apps available to older devices. For the Android Play store to recognize its range of targeted platforms, this needs to be declared in the application's `AndroidManifest.xml` file. This can be found near the top of the project explorer. Include the highlighted code inside the manifest's root node:

```
<uses-sdk
    android:minSdkVersion="16"
    android:targetSdkVersion="23" />
```

If we were to publish this application, it would now appear in the Play store as available to all devices with APIs of 16 or higher.

Applying the material theme

The `AppCompat` library provides a very passable version of material themes, and this is set up in a similar way to the one we encountered in the previous chapter. To see how it's done, start a new Android Studio project with a minimum SDK of 16, create a `colors.xml` file in the `res/values` folder, and complete it as shown as follows:

```
<?xml version="1.0" encoding="utf-8"?>
<resources>
    <color name="primary">#FFC107</color>
    <color name="primary_dark">#FFA000</color>
    <color name="accent">#03A9F4</color>
    <color name="text_primary">#DE000000</color>
    <color name="text_secondary">#8A000000</color>>
</resources>
```

Next, edit the `res/values/styles.xml` file to match the following:

```xml
<resources>
    <style name="AppTheme" parent="Theme.AppCompat.Light">
        <item name="colorPrimary">@color/primary</item>
        <item name="colorPrimaryDark">@color/primary_dark</item>
        <item name="colorAccent">@color/accent</item>
        <item name="android:textColorPrimary">@color/text_primary</item>
        <item name="android:textColor">@color/text_secondary</item>
    </style>
</resources>
```

The fact that our material theme has now been applied can be seen by running the app on a device or emulator running Android 4.1. There are some subtle differences between a true material theme and the one provided by `AppCompat`.

Material design stipulates an important style rule concerning how text is colored. Rather than applying grayscales to emphasize the significance of text, transparency is used as it has a more pleasing effect when placed on colored backgrounds. The rules for text coloring for primary and secondary text, for dark and light backgrounds, are as follows:

- Primary text on a dark background is 87 percent opaque black: `#DE000000`
- Secondary text on a dark background is 54 percent opaque black: `#8A000000`
- Primary text on a light background is 100 percent opaque white: `#FFFFFFFF`
- Secondary text on a light background is 70 percent opaque white: `#B3FFFFFF`

Material Design has quite a few style rules like these, and we will cover them as we go. We have applied our color scheme, but the layout contains the old Action Bar that was replaced, when Material Design was introduced, by the more flexible Toolbar. This has several distinct advantages over its predecessor in that it has more functions, it is not restricted to the top of the screen, and we can have more than one of it.

Adding a material toolbar

To replace the Action Bar with a toolbar, we first have to remove the Action bar. This is easily done by changing the theme in the `res/values/styles.xml` file like this:

```xml
<style name="AppTheme" parent="Theme.AppCompat.Light.NoActionBar">
```

The toolbar can be added by including this tab in the XML activity:

```
<android.support.v7.widget.Toolbar
    android:id="@+id/toolbar"
    android:layout_width="match_parent"
    android:layout_height="56dp"
    android:background="?attr/colorPrimary" />
```

The use of 56dp as the widget's height is not an arbitrary selection; it is another Material Design rule that states that on phones, in portrait mode, the toolbar at the top is 56dp high. This is reduced to 48dp for landscape mode and increased to 64dp for tablets and desktops.

This toolbar is like any other ViewGroup, in that it sits inside the root layout, so unlike the original action bar, it is not plush up to the edges of the screen. To rectify this, open the res/values/dimens.xml/dimens.xml file and change the margin values as shown:

```
<dimen name="activity_horizontal_margin">0dp</dimen>
<dimen name="activity_vertical_margin">0dp</dimen>
```

The toolbar is now positioned and shaded like the original, but has none of the content or function. When a toolbar is given the functionality of the action bar, and is used to access the activity's menu, it is referred to as an App Bar. This is done in the Java element of the activity.

To save time when working with Java, change the settings so that Java libraries are automatically imported when included in code. This is done by navigating to **Editor | General | Auto Import | File | Settings**.

Open the MainActivity.Java file and edit the class declaration so that it extends AppCompatActivity like this:

```
public class MainActivity extends AppCompatActivity {
```

Now, add the highlighted lines, shown here on the onCreate() method:

```
@Override
protected void onCreate(Bundle savedInstanceState) {
    super.onCreate(savedInstanceState);
    setContentView(R.layout.activity_main);
```

```
    Toolbar toolbar = (Toolbar) findViewById(R.id.toolbar);
    if (toolbar != null) {
        setSupportActionBar(toolbar);
    }
}
```

This will generate an error. This is because there are two possible libraries that could be imported here. Press *Alt + Enter* and select the support version of the Toolbar, as shown in the following screenshot:

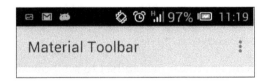

The first of the Java lines we added is a construct that we will come across very often. The `findViewById()` method is used to link instances of views to their Java counterpart.

Testing the project on an emulator running API 16 will immediately demonstrate one of the shortfalls of the `AppCompat` theme; despite declaring a color for our status bar, which works perfectly on API 21 and higher, here it is still black.

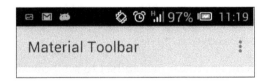

However, this and the absence of natural looking shadows are a small price to pay considering the number of people we can now reach.

Now that we have replaced the old-fashioned Action Bar with a toolbar and set it as the App bar (sometimes called a primary toolbar), we can take a closer look at how it works, and how certain types of icons, known as action icons, are applied according to Material Design rules.

Action icons

As you will be able to see by examining the `MainActivity.Java` code, a rudimentary options menu with a single item has been included, and as we are looking at App bars, now is a great time to introduce the Material Design action icon. Action icons are the small, simple, and single-color icons we are used to seeing on App bars, such as the magnifying glass, search icon, or the hamburger menu icon.

There is no rule against designing your own, but as we haven't yet covered the rules regarding this, and as Google provides a comprehensive and open source collection of material-compliant action icons, it makes a great deal of sense to use those.

Visit `http://www.google.com/design/icons/` and, for the sake of this exercise, download two or three action icons of your choice. Following are the ones used for this exercise:

location.png   sleep.png   time.png

Save these in your project's `drawable` folder and open the `res/menu/menu_main.xml` file. Replace the settings, `<item>`, with ones such as the following one for each icon you have chosen, replacing the highlighted text with values to match your project:

```
<item
    android:id="@+id/menu_date"
    android:icon="@drawable/time"
    android:orderInCategory="100"
    app:showAsAction="always"
    android:title="Date and Time" />
```

You can now test this on an emulator or handset to see how we have replaced the functionality of the action bar.

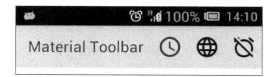

There are a few things that need pointing out here. Icons do not have to appear on the App bar; they can be set to be accessed from the traditional menu icon by changing the value of `app:showAsAction` from `always` to `never` or `ifRoom`. Toolbars can be positioned anywhere on the screen (often at the bottom) by setting the layout gravity property, for example, `android:layout_gravity="bottom|center"`. Toolbars can be given logos, alternative titles, and subtitles with the following Java statements placed after `setActionBar()`, in the next example:

```
getActionBar().setTitle("Clock");
toolbar.setSubtitle("tells the time");
toolbar.setLogo(R.drawable.clock_logo);
```

There are Material Design rules regarding the coloring of action items, which are shaded in the same way as text: by using transparency. These are as follows:

- Action icons on a light background are 54 percent opaque black: `#8A000000`
- Action icons on a dark background are 100 percent opaque white: `#FFFFFF`

We will return to the toolbar time and again, as it is an essential component of Material Design, but as an introduction, this will suffice. Before we return to it, we will become more familiar with other aspects of Material Design.

Summary

A lot of this chapter has not been about Material Design specifically, but we needed to cover this ground to see how Android activities are designed, and how material can be made available to a wider range of devices. This knowledge now enables us to delve deeper into the rules of Material Design that cover color, proportion, and movement.

In the next chapter, we will take this a step further and explore some of the most commonly used material components, including menus, dialogs, and toolbars. We will also see how to include click-listener callback methods that will allow us to respond programmatically to user actions.

3
Common Components

With software installed and a grounding in the principles of Android layout design, we are now in a position to explore the components that make up mobile applications and the material rules that govern their appearance. This chapter covers some of the most common visual components, dialogs, and menus.

After selecting a material-compliant palette, we revisit the toolbar, again using it to replace the old action bar, which is itself a member of the menu family. The Asset Studio is then used to select and configure suitable material icons to represent our menu items and the layout guidelines for phones, tablets, and desktops, which are detailed. The chapter then moves on to actual menus and we construct both the overflow and contextual varieties along with the Java routines required to capture menu events.

This chapter starts to delve further into the code required to develop Android applications. This will involve both XML and Java, although XML is our primary programming tool when it comes to matters of appearance. We will use it to design a custom dialog to material standards lay out our options menu and dictate many of its behaviors. Java is used here to respond to user interaction, mainly in the form of callback methods set in place to be called when our widgets and views are clicked on.

The remainder of this chapter involves creating a custom dialog that adheres to Material Design principles.

In this chapter we will cover the following topics:

- Select a material palette
- Create action icons using Asset Studio
- Learn the material guidelines for app bars
- Capture action calls with Java code
- Create menu layouts and code

- Create a custom alert dialog
- Learn the material guidelines for dialogs
- Use a click listener to capture dialog activity

App bar style and code

This first part of the chapter returns to the app bar, this time looking more closely at the rules and choices as applied to app bar structures and icons. We begin by further examining the ways we can and should customize material themes.

Applying a material palette

Earlier, we touched upon the material theme and how it is possible to customize it and apply our own color scheme. It is perfectly possible to apply any set of colors but Google is quite insistent on how this should be done.

The emphasis with Material Design is on simplicity and using a large number of colors is not recommended. We need just two or three primary shades and one accent shade. Ideally, our palettes should be selected from those found at: `www.google.com/design/spec/style/color.html#color-color-palette`.

Select two of these swatches. One will be used for your primary colors, which will be applied to toolbars and status bars, and the other for the accent color, which will appear in action buttons, sliders, and switches. For this reason, it is important that these colors contrast well. Whichever color you select, the main primary color should have a value of 500 and the darker version should be 700. If you want a lighter version of the primary hue, this should take a value of 100. Select the hue with the value A200 for the accent color. In this example, we used amber for the primary color and light blue for the accent:

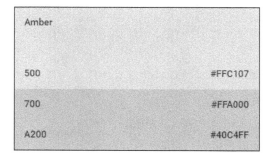

These values should be defined in a file inside the `res/values` directory. This is normally called `colors.xml`, but this is a handy convenience, and you could actually call it anything you chose. The colors in this example, along with text color definitions, would then look like this:

```xml
<?xml version="1.0" encoding="utf-8"?>
<resources>
    <color name="primary">#FFC107</color>
    <color name="primary_dark">#FFA000</color>
    <color name="accent">#40C4FF</color>
    <color name="text_primary">#DE000000</color>
    <color name="text_secondary">#8A000000</color>>
</resources>
```

This can then be used to customize our theme in the `res/values-21/styles.xml` file, as follows:

```xml
<?xml version="1.0" encoding="utf-8"?>
<resources>
    <style name="AppTheme" parent="android:Theme.Material.Light.
NoActionBar">
        <item name="android:colorPrimary">@color/primary</item>
        <item name="android:colorPrimaryDark">@color/primary_dark<//
item>
        <item name="android:colorAccent">@color/accent</item>
        <item name="android:textColorPrimary">@color/text_primary<//
item>
        <item name="android:textColor">@color/text_secondary</item>
    </style>
</resources>
```

If you are developing for older platforms and are using the `AppCompat` library, then the `res/values/styles.xml` file should be completed as well, and should take the following form:

```xml
<?xml version="1.0" encoding="utf-8"?>
<resources>
    <style name="AppTheme" parent="Theme.AppCompat.Light.NoActionBar">
        <item name="colorPrimary">@color/primary</item>
        <item name="colorPrimaryDark">@color/primary_dark</item>
        <item name="colorAccent">@color/accent</item>
        <item name="android:textColorPrimary">@color/text_primary<//
item>
        <item name="android:textColor">@color/text_secondary</item>
    </style>
</resources>
```

Depending on how you created the file, you might have to add compile `'com.android.support:appcompat-v7:22.2.1'` to the `build.gradle` file dependencies, replacing the numbering at the end with whatever revision of the support library you are using. You might also need to adjust the `minSdkVersion` in the `deafaultConfig` section.

Image assets

Next, we are going to replace the action bar with an app bar, as we did in the previous chapter, but here, we will look at it in greater depth and see how its icons can be given functionality using the Java element of the activity.

Open the `res/values/dimens.xml` file and include the following dimensions:

```
<dimen name="toolbar_height">56dp</dimen>
```

Now, instead of adding the toolbar as a widget inside your root layout, create it as a separate resource file by firstly creating a new layout resource from the project explorer.

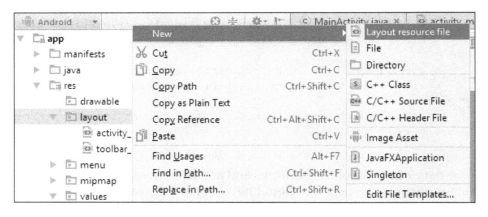

Name the file `toolbar_main` or something similar and fill it out as follows:

```
<?xml version="1.0" encoding="utf-8"?>
<android.support.v7.widget.Toolbar xmlns:android="http://schemas.
android.com/apk/res/android"
    android:id="@+id/toolbar"
    android:layout_width="match_parent"
    android:layout_height="@dimen/toolbar_height"
    android:background="?attr/colorPrimary"
    android:minHeight="?attr/actionBarSize" />
```

This can now be inserted in the appropriate place in your layout with:

```
<include
    layout="@layout/toolbar_main"/>
```

 This technique of creating separate files for individual components is a very handy method; particularly, if we want to use a component in more than one layout.

As before, open the `MainActivity.Java` file and make sure the class extends `AppCompatActivity` and the following lines are added to the `onCreate()` method:

```
Toolbar toolbar = (Toolbar) findViewById(R.id.toolbar);
if (toolbar != null) {
    setSupportActionBar(toolbar);
}
```

In the previous chapter, we added imagery to our projects by placing them in the `drawable` directory, and although this works perfectly well in most cases, the editor comes equipped with a very useful tool for generating images, especially icons, the Asset Studio.

From the `drawable` folder's menu in the project explorer, navigate to **New | Image Asset**. Then, select **Action Bar** and **Tab Icons** as **Asset Type** and then an icon from the collection of clip art:

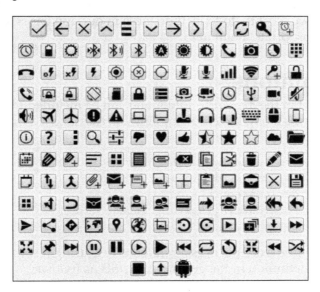

Use the trim and padding options to control the size of the icon, and choose a theme depending on whether your toolbar background color is light or dark. Provide a suitable name and click on **Next**.

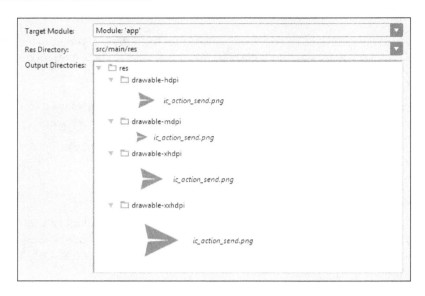

Asset Studio automatically creates icons for us across four screen densities and places them in the correct folders so that they are deployed on the appropriate devices. It even applies the required 54 percent opaque black that Material Design uses for icons. All we have to do to include these in our app bar is to add an icon property to the appropriate menu item.

Applying actions

These icons are kept in the drawable folder and can be included in our menu/action bar by including items along the following lines, in the menu_main.xml file:

```
<item
    android:id="@+id/menu_search"
    android:icon="@drawable/ic_action_search"
    android:orderInCategory="100"
    android:title="@string/search_title"
    app:showAsAction="ifRoom" />
```

Note that the preceding example uses a reference to a string resource, and so must be accompanied by a definition in the strings.xml file as follows:

```
<string name="search_title">Search</string>
```

Menu items are automatically included in the app bar, with the title being taken from the name="app_name" string's definition in the strings file. When constructed in this fashion, these components are positioned according to material guidelines.

The app bar structure

Although the techniques we have applied here conform to material guidelines without us having to do very much other than ensure its height, there will still be times when we are replacing the action bar with a custom toolbar layout, and we will need to know how to space and position the components.

Phones

There are just a few simple structural rules to remember when it comes to app bars. These cover margins and padding, width and height, and positioning; and they differ across platforms and screen orientation.

- layout_height of an app bar in the portrait mode is 56 dp, and 48 dp in landscape.

- App bars fill either the screen width or the width of their containing column. They cannot be divided into two. They have a layout_width of match_parent.

- An app bar has an elevation of 2 dp greater than the sheet of material it controls.

- The exception to the preceding rule is, if a card or dialog has its own toolbar, then the two can share the same elevation.

- App bars have padding of exactly 16 dp. This means the contained icons must have no padding or margins of their own and therefore, share edges with this margin.

- The title text takes its color from your theme's primary text color and the icons from the secondary text.

- The title should be positioned at 72 dp from the left of the toolbar and 20 dp from the bottom. This applies even when the toolbar is expanded.

- The title's text size is set with `android:textAppearance="?android:attr/textAppearanceLarge"`.

Tablets and desktops

When constructing app bars for tablets and desktops, the rules are identical with the following exceptions:

- The toolbar height is always 64 dp
- The title is indented by 80 dp and does not move down when the bar is expanded
- The app bar's padding is 24 dp, with the exception of the top, where it is 20 dp

We have succeeded in constructing an app bar according to material guidelines, but action icons are of no use if they do not perform an action. Next we will see how to interact with our design using Java to provide some functionality.

Capturing action calls with Java code

Very often, an app or activity will have more actions than can reasonably fit on an app bar. The most sensible way to manage this is to have an overflow menu in the form of a drop-down list, but whether the action appears on the app bar or in the options menu, the way we program it is the same. In fact, action icons are really just extensions of the menu. To see how the XML menu works together with Java, start a new project and follow this exercise:

1. Using the Asset Studio, select two action icons as shown in the following screenshot and call them `ic_action_camera` and `ic_action_video`:

2. Replace the action bar with an app bar, as we did earlier in the chapter.

3. Complete the `menu_main.xml` file as follows:

```xml
<menu xmlns:android="http://schemas.android.com/apk/res/android"
    xmlns:app="http://schemas.android.com/apk/res-auto"
    xmlns:tools="http://schemas.android.com/tools"
    tools:context=".MainActivity">

    <item
        android:id="@+id/menu_video"
        android:icon="@drawable/ic_action_video"
        android:orderInCategory="100"
        android:title="Video"
        app:showAsAction="ifRoom" />

    <item
        android:id="@+id/menu_camera"
        android:icon="@drawable/ic_action_camera"
        android:orderInCategory="100"
        android:title="Camera"
        app:showAsAction="ifRoom" />

</menu>
```

4. Open the `MainActivity.Java` file and edit the `onOptionsItemSelected()` method like this:

```java
@Override
public boolean onOptionsItemSelected(MenuItem item) {
    Intent intent;
    int id = item.getItemId();

    switch (id) {
        case R.id.menu_camera:
            intent = new Intent(MediaStore.ACTION_IMAGE_CAPTURE);
            startActivity(intent);
            break;
        case R.id.menu_video:
            intent = new Intent(MediaStore.ACTION_VIDEO_CAPTURE);
            startActivity(intent);
            break;
        default:
            return super.onOptionsItemSelected(item);
    }
}
```

The purpose of this simple example is just to demonstrate how and where menu selections can be captured in Java. The `onOptionsItemSelected(item)` method is a callback method and its code is executed whenever the user selects an item from the options menu.

It is worth taking a moment to examine the example we used here. Intents make up an integral part of any Android app and are abstract operations that are used to start and communicate with other activities. In this case, we used one to start an activity in another app, either the device's native camera app or a choice of applicable installed applications. This process also ensures our activities are placed correctly on the system stack, as can be seen by using the back key from the camera activity or returning to the example after having pressed home from the camera.

We've now seen how to use action icons as options menu items and how they should be styled according to Material Design. There are also guidelines on how menus themselves should be designed, along with a bit of code on how to implement them, and this is what we will take a look at next.

Menus and dialogs

Menus are an important interface in most applications, and although primary actions should always be performed by more obvious means, such as a button, lists of secondary actions are usually best made available through a menu.

When using a material or `AppCompat` theme, most of the material metrics and scales for menus are applied automatically, but occasionally, there are times when we will want to customize a dialog to use as a menu. This section covers how to implement a few common menu features such as submenus, groups, and checkmarks; how to generate popup menus; and finally, how to construct custom dialogs using the material widget, CardView.

Menus

The menus used up until now in this chapter have been designed to demonstrate how an app bar can be used as a menu, but there are times when we want more from such as submenus and menus that are context sensitive. The first thing to do here is to see what more can be done with the app bar overflow menu.

 A complete list of menu elements and syntax can be found at http://developer.android.com/guide/topics/ resources/menu-resource.html.

Options menu

The options menu will conform to material guidelines, aligning, scaling, and coloring text and widgets without us having to do anything at all other than apply a material theme. All that remains is to see how some basic menu functions are implemented.

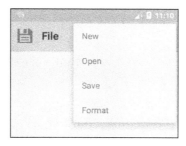

The preceding screenshot shows a menu with four items. The bottom one is actually a simple submenu, which can be seen from the following snippet taken from the main menu XML file:

```
<item
    android:id="@+id/submenu"
    android:orderInCategory="4"
    android:title="Format">
    <menu>
        <item
            android:id="@+id/submenu_word_wrap"
            android:checkable="true"
             android:checked="true"
            android:title="Word wrap" />
        <item
            android:id="@+id/submenu_font"
            android:title="Font" />
    </menu>
</item>
```

Menus can be nested inside each other wherever and however we please, simply by embedding menu nodes inside items. The two highlighted lines in the preceding code demonstrate how an item can have a checkmark provided and set.

Submenu items are handled in Java the same way other app bar and overflow menus are, with the onOptionsItemSelected() method, and the status of the checkmark can be received and set as follows:

```
case R.id.submenu_word_wrap:
    if (item.isChecked()) item.setChecked(false);
    else item.setChecked(true);
    return true;
```

When we want only one item to be selected from a selection, this can be achieved by nesting your selection inside a <group> element, for example:

```
<group android:id="@+id/some_group"
        android:checkableBehavior="single"]
        android:enabled="true" >
    <item
            ... />
    <item
            ... />
</group>
```

> Other values for checkableBehavior are none and all.

The onOptionsItemSelected() callback is a very handy way to manage quite complex menus structures, but there are many times that we want to call a menu from elsewhere in an activity. This can be done with either a popup or a contextual menu. Both are implemented in a very similar fashion, so we shall explore the contextual menu as it is the more interesting of the two.

Contextual menus

Often, we want choices that are specific to an individual component or group rather than an activity or entire app. Android contextual menus perform this function using a long press in the same manner that a right-click is used on a PC. This is performed in a similar manner to the options menu, as can be seen in the following exercise:

1. Start a new project or open one where you have a widget you wish to apply a context menu to. TextView created by the template project will do fine for the sake of this exercise.

2. Create a new menu resource file in the `res/menu` folder called something like `menu_context.xml`, and type in your options, for example:

```xml
<menu xmlns:android="http://schemas.android.com/apk/res/android">
    <item
        android:id="@+id/action_share"
        android:title="Share" />
    <item
        android:id="@+id/action_save"
        android:title="Save" />
    <item
        android:id="@+id/action_delete"
        android:title="Delete" />
</menu>
```

3. Open the `MainActivity` file and include the following lines in the `onCreate()` method:

```java
TextView contextMenu = (TextView) findViewById(R.id.text_view);
registerForContextMenu(contextMenu);
```

4. Add a `onCreateContextMenu()` method to the activity and complete it as follows, inflating the menu we just created:

```java
public void onCreateContextMenu(ContextMenu menu, View view,
ContextMenu.ContextMenuInfo info) {
    super.onCreateContextMenu(menu, view, info);
    MenuInflater inflater = getMenuInflater();
    inflater.inflate(R.menu.menu_context, menu);
```

5. Create another method called `onContextItemSelected()` and fill it out as seen here:

```java
public boolean onContextItemSelected(MenuItem item) {
    AdapterView.AdapterContextMenuInfo info = (AdapterView.
AdapterContextMenuInfo) item.getMenuInfo();
    int id = item.getItemId();

    switch (id) {
        case R.id.action_share:
            doShare(info.id);
            return true;
        case R.id.action_save:
            doSave(info.id);
            return true;
        case R.id.action_delete:
            doDelete(info.id);
            return true;
        default:
            return false;
    }
}
```

6. Routines such as `doShare()`, `doSave()`, and `doDelete()` will of course reflect your own project's purposes, but for the sake of this example, you can use something like the following:

```
private void doShare(long id) {
    Toast.makeText(this, "Shared" + id, Toast.LENGTH_LONG).show();
}
```

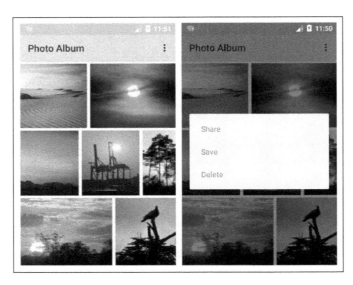

Menus form an essential part of any application whenever a simple selection from a list is required. When slightly more complex decisions are required, we turn to the dialog.

Dialogs

Menus are in the technical sense just a simple form of dialog. Unlike menus, dialogs interrupt the flow of an application, which cannot continue until a choice has been made by the user or the dialog dismissed. For this reason, dialogs must be used sparingly and only when an important decision has to be made.

Dialogs can be generated easily with the SDK and the process explained very quickly. However, from a material perspective, we can learn all we need to know about their structure and appearance by designing a custom dialog.

Dialogs can contain up to three sections: **Title**, **Content**, and **ACTION(S)**.

The following list explains each of these three sections in detail:

- The use of a title requires no explanation. However, for the sake of simplicity, titles should be used only when necessary and should be as brief and succinct as possible.

- Dialog content can vary from a simple list to a date-picker. Alert dialogs, which interrupt user flow, should only ever have one choice or selection.

- Actions confirm a user's choice and should dismiss the dialog once pressed. The number of actions should be kept to a minimum and should generally be affirmative or dismissive, for example **OK** and **CANCEL** or **CONNECT** and **IGNORE**, with the affirmative action always to the right of the dismissive.

Along with this structure comes the usual set of material metrics and there is no better way to learn them than to apply them directly to an XML layout.

Creating a material dialog

In this section, we will create a simple custom alert dialog from scratch, ensuring that it complies with all Material Design guidelines including those regarding touchable targets. The exercise can be carried out on a new project or one that you are working on that requires a dialog:

1. Either open or start a project and apply your custom colors and theme.

2. Navigate to **New | Layout resource file** in the `layout` folder with a **LinearLayout** root, called something like `dialog_example.xml`.

3. Using the design interface, generate the following layout:

4. Now, locate the method that you will be using to call the dialog (you can use `onCreate()` for testing purposes) and add the following lines:

```
final Dialog dialog = new Dialog(this);
dialog.setContentView(R.layout.dialog_example);
dialog.show();
```

If you were to compile and run the project now, you would see that there is an unexplained space at the top of the widget. This is because the title is included, by default, as part of the `Dialog` object. We could use this, rather than create our own by including a call to its `setTitle()` method, for example, `dialog.setTitle(R.string.dialog_title)`. For now, we will remove it and use our custom layout to define the title. This can be done by inserting the following line before the call to `setContentView()`:

```
dialog.requestWindowFeature(Window.FEATURE_NO_TITLE);
```

To best understand the content guidelines, we will take each of the three elements one by one.

Title

The padding around the title is `24dp`, with the space underneath being `20dp`. This, along with the correct text settings, can be defined as:

```
<TextView
    android:id="@+id/text_title"
    android:layout_width="wrap_content"
    android:layout_height="wrap_content"
    android:paddingBottom="20dp"
    android:paddingLeft="24dp"
    android:paddingRight="24dp"
    android:paddingTop="24dp"
    android:text="@string/dialog_title"
    android:textAppearance="?android:attr/textAppearanceLarge"
    android:textColor="@color/text_primary" />
```

Content

Formatting the content is even simpler as it too has a padding around it of `24dp` and the `20dp` space between it and the title has already been taken care of. The XML rendition looks like this:

```
<TextView
    android:id="@+id/text_content"
    android:layout_width="wrap_content"
```

```
    android:layout_height="wrap_content"
    android:paddingBottom="24dp"
    android:paddingLeft="24dp"
    android:paddingRight="24dp"
    android:text="@string/dialog_content"
    android:textAppearance="?android:attr/textAppearanceSmall"
    android:textColor="@color/text_secondary" />
```

Actions

The layout of the action section of an alert dialog poses a far more interesting challenge than merely learning the correct margins, not to help those among us with fat thumbs, the touchable target area for the buttons must be larger than the button itself. There are several solutions to this conundrum, but let's first define the action area itself.

The design guidelines stipulate that the action section must be 52dp high with an 8dp padding on all sides. The buttons themselves are aligned on the right but gravity is set to the end rather than the right, so as to cater to those locales where content is read from right to left. All this can be achieved with the following entry:

```
<LinearLayout
    android:layout_width="match_parent"
    android:layout_height="52dp"
    android:gravity="center_vertical|end"
    android:orientation="horizontal"
    android:padding="8dp">
```

This brings us to the buttons. These must be none narrower than 64dp, which is easily managed with the android:minWidth property, as is the height of 36dp and the 8dp margin between buttons. The interesting part comes when deciding how to make buttons with a height of 36dp have a touchable height of 48dp. One way of handling this is with the TouchDelegate class, which is very effective but can take some coming to grips with. For those with an interest, the documentation can be found at http://developer.android.com/reference/android/view/TouchDelegate.html. Another method would be to embed each button in a larger clickable ViewGroup. This works equally well but the additional layouts will have an unnecessary effect on performance.

The solution we will use here is to use TextViews instead of buttons. The issue of an expanded touchable target is instantly resolved, as we simply make the text views 48 dp high, plus there is no need for extra coding, layouts, customizing themes, or removing button borders.

Buttons can be made borderless with the this attribute:
`style="?android:attr/borderlessButtonStyle"`.

All this, along with the guideline that buttons must never be narrower than `64dp`, can be expressed in XML as:

```
<TextView
    android:id="@+id/text_remove"
    android:layout_width="wrap_content"
    android:layout_height="wrap_content"
    android:height="48dp"
    android:clickable="true"
    android:gravity="center_vertical|center_horizontal"
    android:minWidth="64dp"
    android:text="@string/remove"
    android:textAppearance="?android:attr/textAppearanceSmall"
    android:textColor="@color/accent" />
```

Both buttons have identical markup with the obvious exception of the text itself. Calling `dialog.show()` should now render a dialog like this:

This might seem like a lot of effort to go to in order to produce a dialog that could have been generated for us, and commands such as `dialog.setTitle(String)` and `.setContent(String)` are the more obvious route if all we need is a standard dialog; although, we could have used the base class `AlertDialog` rather than `Dialog`. Doing it this way is not only a great way to become acquainted with the guidelines but also leads the way to creating original designs that still comply with material guidelines.

 Although it is set automatically here, for your reference, dialogs have an elevation of `48dp`.

Click listeners

None of this is of any use if we cannot connect the dialog to some procedural code. This can be done in two ways. Firstly, the method to be called can be specified in any view from its XML markup. This can be done with:

```
android:onClick="someMethod"
```

Here, someMethod() is defined in the corresponding Java activity.

Alternatively, a click listener can be implemented in Java that will be called whenever the button is clicked. In the preceding example and in the same method that you used to call the dialog, create a reference to the XML view you want to respond to as follows:

```
TextView cancelButton = (TextView) dialog.findViewById(R.id.text_
cancel);
```

Then, create this onClickListener:

```
cancelButton.setOnClickListener(new View.OnClickListener() {

    @Override
    public void onClick(View v) {
        dialog.dismiss();
    }
});
```

> The listener here is a great way to respond to a single button, but in cases where an activity has several, it is a better idea to implement an onClickListener for the whole class, which can be done with the public class MainActivity extends Activity implements View.OnClickListener and then handle all click events for the activity from the onClick() method.

With the knowledge of how to construct and code material-compliant dialogs, we can conclude our brief look around three of the most commonly used application components and move on to components more commonly associated with Material Design.

Summary

Dialogs and menus form an integral part of any application, in particular on mobile platforms where space is limited. As always, the material approach is to keep these clean and simple, in content as well as appearance. We have seen what the guidelines are and how they can be applied with XML, as well as seeing how these interfaces connect to and are controlled by our Java code.

Dialogs and menus are elements of most applications and are by no means peculiar to Material Design and this chapter has covered only the visual aspects. There are of course many screen components that are specific to Material Design such as the floating action button and navigation drawer, many of which are catered to in a support library of their own, the design library.

In the next chapter, we will explore the way users navigate around an Android app. This will involve creating a sliding navigation drawer and the use of fragments to display alternative content. We will also cover ratios and designing for varying screen densities.

4
Sliding Drawers and Navigation

In the previous chapter, we saw how Material Design applies to several everyday app components, and when designing material interfaces, you will, no doubt, include these along with many other general purpose widgets and views. There are some components, however, that are specific to Material Design, such as the sliding navigation drawer that we will be dealing with in this chapter. Regardless of side, drawers appear above all other components with the exception of the status and navigation bars. They can be thought of as existing just off screen. They can be thought of as existing just off screen as demonstrated by the following diagram:

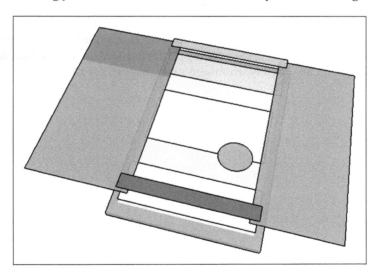

Two support libraries are required to set up the siding navigation drawer: the v4 library and the design library. Of all the support libraries supplied by the SDK, it is the design library that is, perhaps, the most useful to the material designer. Where before, a great deal of coding was required to construct material components from existing ones, the design library makes them available as classes in their own right, which allows us to include them in our layouts and code, just as we would any other view or view group.

In this chapter we are going to discuss the following topics:

- Create a working navigation drawer
- Design a header
- Build a navigation menu
- Understand ratio keylines
- Design for a range of screen densities
- Activate the navigation drawer
- Use fragments
- Build other types of sliding drawers

Drawer design

Some of the most useful and frequently used material components are sliding drawers that slide in and out of the screen when needed. The most widely used of these is the **NavigationView**, which slides in from the left and forms a top level menu, providing access to the rest of the app's content. More often than not, it will contain a header that can display an image and/or pertinent text.

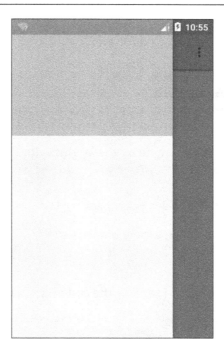

Prior to the design library, components like the NavigationView had to be constructed from other views, and although the library vastly simplifies this process and saves us from having to implement many material principles by hand, there are still several guidelines that we need to be aware of. The best way to appreciate these guidelines is by building a navigation sliding drawer from scratch. This will involve creating the layouts, applying material guidelines regarding component ratios, and connecting all this together with Java.

The layout

Setting up a working sliding drawer with a header and NavigationView is a little more involved than the components we have dealt with so far, and it is not easy to test until quite a bit of code has been entered and resources have been provided. We will start by setting up the project and constructing the main XML layout:

1. Start a new Android Studio project and provide it with your own customized colors and theme.

2. Add the following line to your `styles.xml` file:

```
<item name="android:statusBarColor">@android:color/transparent</item>
```

3. Open the `Gradle Scripts build.gradle (Module: app)` file and add the highlighted dependencies that follow:

```
dependencies {
    compile fileTree(dir: 'libs', include: ['*.jar'])
    compile 'com.android.support:appcompat-v7:22.2.1'
    compile 'com.android.support:design:22.2.1'
}
```

4. In the `layout` directory, create a new layout called `toolbar.xml` and complete it as shown here:

```xml
<?xml version="1.0" encoding="utf-8"?>
<android.support.v7.widget.Toolbar xmlns:android="http://schemas.
android.com/apk/res/android"
    android:layout_width="match_parent"
    android:layout_height="56dp"
    android:background="@color/primary" />
```

5. Open `activity_main` and replace the code with the following lines:

```xml
<android.support.v4.widget.DrawerLayout xmlns:android="http://
schemas.android.com/apk/res/android"
    xmlns:app="http://schemas.android.com/apk/res-auto"
    xmlns:tools="http://schemas.android.com/tools"
    android:id="@+id/drawer"
    android:layout_width="match_parent"
    android:layout_height="match_parent"
    android:fitsSystemWindows="true"
    tools:context=".MainActivity">

    <LinearLayout
        android:layout_width="match_parent"
        android:layout_height="match_parent"
        android:orientation="vertical">

        <include
            android:id="@+id/toolbar"
            layout="@layout/toolbar" />

        <FrameLayout
            android:id="@+id/fragment"
            android:layout_width="match_parent"
            android:layout_height="match_parent">
        </FrameLayout>

    </LinearLayout>
```

```
<android.support.design.widget.NavigationView
    android:id="@+id/navigation_view"
    android:layout_width="wrap_content"
    android:layout_height="match_parent"
    android:layout_gravity="start"
    app:headerLayout="@layout/header"
    app:menu="@menu/menu_drawer" />

</android.support.v4.widget.DrawerLayout>
```

As you can see, the root layout here is DrawerLayout, as provided by the support library. Note the fitsSystemWindows property; this is what makes the drawer extend up to the top of the screen under the status bar. Having set the statusBarColor option to android:color/transparent in the style, the drawer is now visible through the status bar:

 This effect is not available on devices running Android versions older than 5.0 (API 21), even with AppCompat, and this will alter the apparent aspect ratio of the header and clip any images. To counter this, create an alternative styles.xml resource that does not set the fitsSystemWindows property.

The rest of the layout consists of a LinearLayout and NavigationView itself. The linear layout contains our app bar and an empty FrameLayout. FrameLayouts are the simplest of layouts, containing only a single item, and are generally used as a placeholder, which in this case will contain content based on the user's selection from the navigation menu.

This defines our sliding drawer rather well, but we still need to provide the header, along with the menu highlighted in the main activity that was previously mentioned.

Navigation components and keylines

As mentioned earlier, side navigation views usually contain a header and a menu. We are familiar with menus and how they operate, but there are aspects of the header, which as material designers, we need to know about. In particular, the way that specific aspect ratios are used to define where borders between certain components, known as ratio keylines, are allowed and need to be adhered to, and how this is managed across devices with varying screen densities. Next, we will provide the XML for both components, and then explain the structure, followed by ratio keylines and how they are implemented.

Structure and metrics

The header and menu components are entered as files, separate from the main activity code. Follow these steps to implement them:

1. Create a **New** in the `Menu resource` file in the `menu` directory called `menu_drawer.xml` and fill it out as shown:

```xml
<?xml version="1.0" encoding="utf-8"?>
<menu xmlns:android="http://schemas.android.com/apk/res/android">

    <item
        android:id="@+id/drama"
        android:icon="@drawable/drama"
        android:title="@string/drama" />
    <item
        android:id="@+id/film"
        android:icon="@drawable/film"
        android:title="@string/film" />

    <item
        android:id="@+id/sport"
        android:icon="@drawable/sport"
        android:title="@string/sport" />

    <item
        android:id="@+id/news"
        android:title="@string/news">
        <menu>
            <item
                android:id="@+id/national"
                android:icon="@drawable/news"
                android:title="@string/national" />
```

```
            <item
                android:id="@+id/sub2"
                android:icon="@drawable/international"
                android:title="@string/international" />

        </menu>
    </item>
</menu>
```

2. Find appropriate icons for each item and place them in your `drawable` directory.

3. Place an image called `header_background` in the `drawable` directory. The size is not important here, but ensure that the image ratio is 4:3, for example, 640 x 480.

4. Create another layout resource file called `header.xml` and fill it out as shown here:

```
<?xml version="1.0" encoding="utf-8"?>
<RelativeLayout xmlns:android="http://schemas.android.com/apk/res/
android"
    android:layout_width="match_parent"
    android:layout_height="192dp"
    android:background="@drawable/header_background"
    android:orientation="vertical">

    <TextView
        android:id="@+id/feature"
        android:layout_width="wrap_content"
        android:layout_height="wrap_content"
        android:layout_above="@+id/details"
        android:gravity="left"
        android:paddingBottom="8dp"
        android:paddingLeft="16dp"
        android:text="@string/feature"
        android:textColor="#FFFFFF"
        android:textSize="14sp"
        android:textStyle="bold" />

    <TextView
        android:id="@+id/details"
        android:layout_width="wrap_content"
        android:layout_height="wrap_content"
        android:layout_alignStart="@+id/feature"
        android:layout_alignParentBottom="true"
        android:layout_marginBottom="16dp"
        android:gravity="left"
        android:paddingLeft="16dp"
```

```
        android:text="@string/details"
        android:textColor="#FFFFFF"
        android:textSize="14sp" />

    </RelativeLayout>
```

The menu is similar to those we have already seen, and you need not make your menu as long as the one here, but make sure that you include a sub-menu, as these are displayed differently when it comes to navigation drawers.

Most of the metrics of sliding drawers and navigation views, such as margins and text sizes, are taken care of for us, thanks to the design library. However, the size, position, and color of text on a drawer header are not. Despite sharing a background, the text should be thought of as a 56 dp high component in its own right. It should have an internal padding of 16 dp and 8 dp of spacing between the lines. This, along with the correct text color, size, and weight can be derived from the preceding code.

The height of the header, 192 dp, may well seem puzzling and requires some explanation as to how it was calculated. Generally, the use of density-independent pixels saves us having to concern ourselves with target screen densities. There are times, however, when we need to take this into consideration if we want our apps to conform to material guidelines.

Ratio keylines

When an element, such as a sliding drawer, fills the entire height of a screen and is divided into vertical segments, as our drawer is, between header and content, these divisions can occur only at certain points known as ratio keylines. These points are determined by the ratio between the width of the element and how far from the top the division occurs. There are six such ratios allowed in material layouts, and they are defined as width to height (`width:height`) and are as follows:

```
16:9
3:2
4:3
1:1
3:4
2:3
```

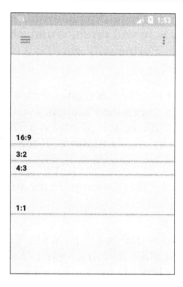

In the example here, a 4:3 ratio was chosen, the width of the drawer being 256 dp. We could also have produced a header with a 16:9 ratio and set `layout_height` at `144dp`.

Ratio keylines only relate to the distance from the top of the containing element; you cannot have one 16:9 view below another. However, you can place one view beneath another, if it extends from the bottom of that view down to another of the ratio keylines.

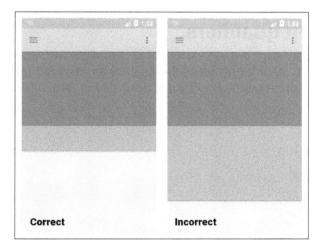

Having understood the guidelines regarding allowed ratios, we can now look at why setting `layout_height` in this way will produce undesirable results when tested across varying screen densities. Fortunately, there is a convenient solution to this situation.

As covered briefly in an earlier chapter, Android uses a universal pixel unit: the device-independent pixel. This uses a base scale of 160 dpi. This means that a 100 x 100 dp view would cover 200 x 200 actual pixels on a 320 dpi device. Although this system works reasonably well in most situations, it falls down if we want to maintain ratio keylines.

There is a simple formula to calculate dp from px for any given screen density:

```
dp = ( px x 160 ) / dpi
```

Say that we have a 240 dpi screen that is 480 px wide. This would translate into a screen that was 320 dp wide. Three-quarters of this would be 240 dp and we could use this to generate a 4:3 layout. As you can see, different screen densities will yield different results, and the height of 192 dp that we used here will only produce a 4:3 image when the layout containing it is 256 dp wide, which is only the case on a 240 dpi device.

The ratios recommended in Material Design are not selected arbitrarily. They are, in fact, derived from traditional design paradigms and are considered universally pleasing to the human eye, even the tiniest distortion can completely ruin this effect. Fortunately, ensuring that these ratios are maintained across all devices is not a difficult task, as we shall see next.

Configuration qualifiers

Android devices come with a wide variety of screen densities, and it would be impossible to cater to all of them. Instead, densities are divided into six categories, which, in almost all circumstances, produce desirable results. These categories are as follows:

- **ldpi**: 120 dpi
- **mdpi**: 160 dpi
- **hdpi**: 240 dpi
- **xhdpi**: 320 dpi
- **xxhdpi**: 480 dpi
- **xxxhdpi**: 640 dpi

It is, of course, a simple matter to calculate the correct height for any view at any density, for example, on a 320 dpi device the drawer would equate it to 192 dp wide, and so we would have to set the header `layout_width` to `144dp`.

The solution is to create separate resources for each density grouping. Fortunately, we do not need to recreate the entire layout for each density, but only the `dimens.xml` file. This is achieved through the use of configuration qualifiers in the directory names.

To see how this is done, complete the following steps:

1. Open the `res/dimens.xml/dimens.xml` file and add the following line:

   ```
   <dimen name="header_height">192dp</dimen>
   ```

2. Change the `layout_height` definition in the header:

   ```
   android:layout_height="@dimen/header_height"
   ```

3. Create six new folders in your `res` directory called `values-ldpi`, `values-mdpi`, and so on.

4. Create a `dimens.xml` file in each of these folders. The `New thingy resource` dialog will allow you to select the relevant directory that will not be visible in the project explorer right away.

5. Calculate the correct `header_height` for each density group and include this in each `dimens` file. For example:

   ```
   <resources>
       <dimen name="header_height">144dp</dimen>
   </resources>
   ```

 A very similar process can be applied when it comes to scaling images for a range of pixel densities. This can ensure high-quality images on devices capable of displaying them without using up memory unnecessarily on less sophisticated devices. This can be achieved with qualified `drawable` directories, for example, `drawable-xhdpi`. The scaling required for any given density is easily calculated as *dpi/160*.

We have created our sliding drawer along with a header and NavigationView, and ensured that ratio keylines are adhered to across most screen densities. However, we still cannot see it. To do so, we will need to connect it all together with Java.

Drawer functionality

Many recent widgets and views are not viewable using Android Studio's preview or design modes, and although there are frequent updates to rectify these issues, there will always be times when the only way to view a layout is to run it on an emulator or device. As it stands, the code we have will not compile until we enter the Java code explained in the following two parts of the exercise. Firstly, we will connect our app bar, drawer, and navigation view, and secondly, we will see how to link navigation items to the rest of our apps. The chapter concludes with a look at alternative ways to implement sliding drawers.

Activating the navigation drawer

Once the following code has been entered, it will be possible to view and test your navigation bar:

1. Open the `MainActivity` file and add the following lines in the `onCreate()` method to replace the action bar with our toolbar:

    ```
    toolbar = (Toolbar) findViewById(R.id.toolbar);
    setSupportActionBar(toolbar);
    ```

2. Beneath this, add the following lines to configure the drawer:

    ```
    drawerLayout = (DrawerLayout) findViewById(R.id.drawer);
    ActionBarDrawerToggle toggle = new ActionBarDrawerToggle(this,
    drawerLayout, toolbar, R.string.openDrawer, R.string.closeDrawer)
    {

    @Override
    public void onDrawerOpened(View v) {
        // YOUR CODE HERE
        super.onDrawerOpened(v);
    }

    @Override
    public void onDrawerClosed(View v) {
        // YOUR CODE HERE
        super.onDrawerClosed(v);
    }

    };

    drawerLayout.setDrawerListener(toggle);
    toggle.syncState();
    ```

3. Finally, add this code to set up the navigation view:

```
navigationView = (NavigationView) findViewById(R.id.navigation_
view);

navigationView.setNavigationItemSelectedListener(new
NavigationView.OnNavigationItemSelectedListener() {

    @Override
    public boolean onNavigationItemSelected(MenuItem item) {
        drawerLayout.closeDrawers();

        switch (item.getItemId()) {
            case R.id.drama:
                Toast.makeText(getApplicationContext(), "drama",
Toast.LENGTH_SHORT).show();
                return true;
            case R.id.film:
                Toast.makeText(getApplicationContext(), "film",
Toast.LENGTH_SHORT).show();
                return true;
            case R.id.news:
                Toast.makeText(getApplicationContext(), "news",
Toast.LENGTH_SHORT).show();
                return true;
            case R.id.sport:
                Toast.makeText(getApplicationContext(), "sport",
Toast.LENGTH_SHORT).show();
                return true;
            default:
                return true;
            }
        }
    });
```

The preceding Java code allows us to view our drawer on a device or emulator, but it does very little when a navigation item is selected. What we really need, actually, is to be taken to another part of the app. This is very simply achieved and we will come to it in a moment. First, there are one or two points in the previous code that require mentions.

The line beginning with `ActionBarDrawerToggle` is what causes the hamburger that opens the drawer to appear on the app bar, although you can, of course, open it with an inward swipe from the left of the screen. The two string arguments, `openDrawer` and `closeDrawer`, are there for reasons of accessibility, and are read out for users who are unable to see the screen clearly. They should say something like *Navigation drawer opening* and *Navigation drawer closing*. The two callback methods, `onDrawerOpened()` and `onDrawerClosed()`, were left empty here simply to demonstrate where these events can be intercepted to trigger further code.

`OnNavigationItemSelectedListener()` is very similar to the other listeners we have encountered. The call to `drawerLayout.closeDrawers()` is essential, as otherwise, the drawer would remain open. As it stands, the response is a simple pop-up message. Obviously, what we want is for the menu to direct us to another part of the application. This is not a difficult task and also provides a good opportunity to introduce one of the SDK's most useful and versatile classes: the **fragment**.

Opening fragments

From what we have learned so far, it would be safe to imagine that separate activities would be used for apps with more than one function, and although this is often the case, it can be an expensive drain on resources and activities always filling the entire screen. Fragments operate like mini-activities, in that they have both Java and XML definitions, and fragments also have many of the same callbacks and functionality that activities do. Unlike activities, fragments are not top-level components and must reside within a host activity. The advantage of this is that we can have more than one fragment per screen.

As it is simply for show, we will be doing no coding for this particular fragment, and we need to do little more than set up the class itself. Create a new Java class called `ContentFragment` and complete it as shown in the following lines, making sure you import `android.support.v4.app.Fragment` rather than the standard version:

```
public class ContentFragment extends Fragment {

    @Override
    public View onCreateView(LayoutInflater inflater, ViewGroup
container, Bundle savedInstanceState) {
        View v = inflater.inflate(R.layout.content,container,false);
        return v;
    }

}
```

As for the XML element, create a layout file called `content.xml` and place whatever views and widgets you choose inside it. All that is needed now is the Java code to call it when a navigation item is selected.

Open the `MainActivity.Java` file and replace one of the toasts in the `switch` statement with this code:

```
ContentFragment fragment = new ContentFragment();
android.support.v4.app.FragmentTransaction transaction =
getSupportFragmentManager().beginTransaction();
transaction.replace(R.id.fragment, fragment);
transaction.addToBackStack(null);
transaction.commit();
```

The example we have built here is solely to demonstrate the basic anatomy of drawer layouts and NavigationViews. Clearly, to add any real functionality, we would need a fragment for each item in our menu, and the line, `transaction.addToBackStack(null)`, is actually redundant unless we do so. Its function is to ensure that the order in which a user accesses each fragment is recorded by the system in the same way it records which activities are used so that when they press the back key, they will return to the previous fragment. Without it, they would be returned to the previous application.

The NavigationView is an essential component of many material applications, but it is not the only use of sliding drawers, nor is it necessary to have a drawer slide in and out from the left.

Other sliding drawers

Although it is quite possible to have the NavigationView slide in from the right, it should always be kept to the left as this provides a consistent experience for users. There are times, however, when another sliding drawer would suit our purposes, and this is easily achieved; although right-sided drawers should not be used for primary or top level actions, but rather as a convenient method of accessing secondary functions such as volume controls or share options. The following image demonstrates how the right-sided drawer relates to the other screen components:

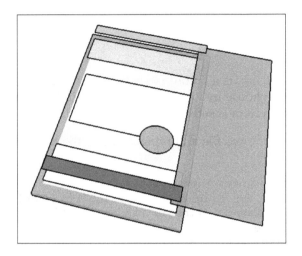

Unlike the left-sided navigation drawer that is never wider than the screen width minus the primary toolbar's height, a right-sided drawer can extend all the way across the screen.

Creating a drawer that slides in and out from the right requires nothing more than setting the content's `layout_gravity` option, which can be seen by adding this view to the `activity_main` layout in the same node as the NavigationView:

```
<ListView
    android:id="@+id/right_drawer"
    android:layout_width="180dp"
    android:layout_height="match_parent"
    android:layout_gravity="end"
    android:background="@color/primary_dark" />
```

There is a lot more to be said about sliding drawers and navigation, but as far as it goes for setting them up and understanding what is required to adhere to Material Design guidelines, we have done enough to be getting on with.

Summary

We have seen in this chapter how to put together a sliding navigation drawer using DrawerLayout from the v4 support library and the NavigationView from the design library. In doing this, we have learned about the permitted aspect ratios that are allowed on full-length view groups. We have seen how qualifying directory names can help us develop resources that can cater to all kinds of device configurations, how all this can be brought to life using Java, and how fragments provide a simple and efficient way to provide as many screens and layouts as our app might require.

In the next chapter, we will be taking a little bit of an artistic detour and exploring the iconography and typography of Material Design, and how we can apply these concepts to our own applications.

5
Lists, Cards, and Data

Modern smartphones and tablets are capable of accessing and managing large amounts of data, and due to the limited screen space on most of these devices, handling large data sets poses an interesting challenge. Prior to Android 5, these data sets were usually handled with ListView, but this was notoriously inefficient and so Android 5 introduced RecyclerView, which intelligently manages large lists and grids.

RecyclerView is also more flexible than ListView, as we can create custom layouts for individual lists or grid items, and one of the best ways to achieve this is with CardView, which also came out with Android 5 and has become synonymous with Material Design.

As we see how these views are implemented, we will also take a deeper look at what has to be the material designer's most useful tool: the design support library. In particular, we will be using CoordinatorLayout, which automates many material functions such as swipe-to-dismiss and animations.

In this chapter we will cover the following topics:

- Applying new support libraries
- Implementing CoordinatorLayout
- Using RecyclerView to produce lists
- Managing data with an adapter
- Learning typographical rules
- Implementing CardViews and tiles

Generating lists

There is quite a lot of code involved in putting these components together, and the best way to see how this is done is to get straight down to it:

1. Create a new project in Android Studio and apply a material theme by creating a `colors.xml` file and editing the style files to apply it. You will need to ensure that you have the following dependencies applied in your `build.gradle` file:

    ```
    dependencies {
    compilefileTree(dir: 'libs', include: ['*.jar'])
    compile 'com.android.support:appcompat-v7:23.0.0'
    compile 'com.android.support:design:23.0.0'
    compile 'com.android.support:recyclerview-v7:23.0.0'
    compile 'com.android.support:cardview-v7:23.0.0'
    }
    ```

2. As before, create a separate toolbar layout called `toolbar.xml`, along the lines of the code here:

    ```
    <?xml version="1.0" encoding="utf-8"?>
    <android.support.v7.widget.Toolbarxmlns:android="http://schemas.
    android.com/apk/res/android"
    android:layout_width="match_parent"
    android:layout_height="56dp"
    android:background="@color/primary" />
    ```

3. Include the toolbar in your `activity_main.xml` layout, like so:

    ```
    <include
    android:id="@+id/toolbar"
        layout="@layout/toolbar" />
    ```

4. Then, replace the action bar by using `.NoActionBar` in the theme of your choice and adding the following lines to the `onCreate()` method of the `MainActivity.java` file:

    ```
    Toolbar toolbar = (Toolbar) findViewById(R.id.toolbar);
    if (toolbar != null) {
    setSupportActionBar(toolbar);
      }
    ```

These previous steps are something that we will generally have to do every time we start a new project, and as such, will not be referred to again here.

`CoordinatorLayout` is an extremely useful tool that simplifies and automates many material features, as its name suggests, by coordinating the child views and widgets it contains. It is very simple to apply to our main layout XML file; simply add the code here, beneath where you have included the toolbar:

```
<android.support.design.widget.CoordinatorLayout
xmlns:android="http://schemas.android.com/apk/res/android"
xmlns:app="http://schemas.android.com/apk/res-auto"
android:id="@+id/content"
android:layout_width="match_parent"
android:layout_height="match_parent"
android:layout_below="@+id/toolbar">

</android.support.design.widget.CoordinatorLayout>
```

RecyclerView can be placed inside the `CoordinatorLayour`, like so:

```
<android.support.v7.widget.RecyclerView
android:id="@+id/list"
android:layout_width="match_parent"
android:layout_height="match_parent" />
```

The editor fills RecyclerView with dummy data so that we can preview our activity, but to populate it with actual data we will need to set up a layout manager and a data adapter. First, we need to decide what data we want to represent. This we will do using CardView, which has become a ubiquitous part of Material Design, a typical example of which can be seen here:

Adding list items

To keep things simple, we will create cards with a small image and two lines of text, similar to what we might find in a contact list. There is quite a lot of code to this layout, but it gives us the opportunity to apply Material Design spacing and text. Following is the complete listing with definitions that pertain particularly to material being highlighted:

```xml
<?xml version="1.0" encoding="utf-8"?>
<LinearLayoutxmlns:android="http://schemas.android.com/apk/res/
android"
xmlns:card_view="http://schemas.android.com/apk/res-auto"
android:layout_width="match_parent"
android:layout_height="match_parent">

<android.support.v7.widget.CardView
android:id="@+id/card_view"
android:layout_width="match_parent"
android:layout_height="wrap_content">

<RelativeLayout
android:layout_width="match_parent"
android:layout_height="wrap_content"
android:padding="16dp">

<ImageView
android:id="@+id/profile_pic"
android:layout_width="wrap_content"
android:layout_height="wrap_content"
android:layout_alignParentLeft="true"
android:layout_alignParentTop="true"
android:layout_marginRight="16dp" />

<TextView
android:id="@+id/name"
android:layout_width="wrap_content"
android:layout_height="wrap_content"
android:layout_alignParentTop="true"
android:layout_toRightOf="@+id/profile_pic"
android:textSize="24sp" />

<TextView
android:id="@+id/status"
android:layout_width="wrap_content"
android:layout_height="wrap_content"
```

```
android:layout_below="@+id/name"
android:textSize="16sp"
android:layout_toRightOf="@+id/profile_pic" />

</RelativeLayout>

</android.support.v7.widget.CardView>

</LinearLayout>
```

Although we cannot view this layout until we have linked it together with the data we want to use, it should be clear from the XML that we have created a layout that will look like the following one:

Before we create our data, there are one or two things that need pointing out about this new class. Firstly, CardViews have their corners rounded and their elevation set automatically to comply with material guidelines. However, it is often useful to be able to set these manually with XML, and this can be done with the following commands:

```
card_view:cardElevation="4dp"
card_view:cardCornerRadius="6dp"
```

Neither of these properties will work on Android versions prior to 5.0 and alternative layouts are usually required, although there is a very handy method of determining the SDK version during runtime. When you wish to set the elevation, where possible, but ignore the command on older devices, the following clause can be used:

```
if (Build.VERSION.SDK_INT>= Build.VERSION_CODES.LOLLIPOP) {
someWidget.setElevation(4);
}
```

You may notice that some margins and padding look different on CardViews when tested on older versions. Rather than resort to creating alternative layout resources, the `card_view:cardUseCompatPadding="true"` property will often resolve this.

Text size is very important when it comes to Material Design and only certain sizes are permitted in certain contexts. In the current example, we selected 24 sp for the header text and 16 for the subhead. Generally speaking, nearly all the text we will ever display in a Material Design application will be 12, 14, 16, 20, or 34 scalable pixels. There is a certain level of flexibility when it comes to selecting which size to use and when, but the following image should provide a good guide:

Display 1: Regular 34sp
Headline: Regular 24sp
Title: Medium 20sp
Subhead: Regular 16sp
Body 2: Medium 14sp
Body 1: Regular 14sp
Caption: Regular 12sp
Button: MEDIUM ALL CAPS 14sp

On the rare occasions that you might need a larger font, you should select from 45, 56, or 112 sp, the largest of these being Roboto light.

It is always well worth taking into account that the use of scalable pixels is intended to allow users to set the font size on their devices to suit their own needs, and that very often you will have no control over how text is actually rendered on a downloaded app.

As you will know, Google developed the Roboto family of fonts for material applications, and it has been designed specifically for its style and readability on handheld devices. It can be downloaded from `https://www.google.com/fonts/specimen/Roboto`.

Connecting a dataset

Android comes equipped with the SQLite library, which is a powerful tool for creating and managing complex databases. One could easily fill an entire chapter, or even a whole book, on the subject, but as this does not really bear any relation to Material Design, we will create a very simple dataset just so that we can test out our RecyclerView.

If you would like to learn more about SQLite, comprehensive documentation can be found at `http://developer.android.com/reference/android/database/sqlite/SQLiteDatabase.html`.

For the sake of brevity, the example here contains only three entries; however, it is very easy to expand if you choose. To add this data, create a new Java class called `Contact.Java` and complete like so:

```
public class Contact {
intprofilePic;
    String name;
    String status;
private List<Contact> contacts;

Contact(intprofilePic, String name, String status) {
this.profilePic = profilePic;
this.name = name;
this.status = status;
    }

private void loadData() {
contacts = new ArrayList<>();
contacts.add(new Contact(R.drawable.picture01, "Bill", "Currently
offline"));
contacts.add(new Contact(R.drawable.picture02, "Sally", "Currently
busy"));
contacts.add(new Contact(R.drawable.picture03, "Janet", "Available to
chat"));
    }
}
```

As you can see, you will require some images for this exercise. The images selected for demonstration were 64 x 64 dp. This means that you will need to scale these up for higher density devices. For example, the xxhdpi version will need to be 256 x 256 actual pixels.

Although RecyclerView is a fantastic tool for managing and binding data in an efficient manner, it does require quite a bit of setting up. Apart from the view and the data, there are two other elements required to bind the data to our view: LayoutManager and the data adapter.

Layout managers and adapters

As already mentioned, RecyclerViews manage their data using `RecyclerView.LayoutManager` and `RecyclerView.Adapter`. LayoutManager can be thought of as belonging to RecyclerView and it is this that communicates with the adapter, which in turn is bound to our data in a fashion depicted in the following figure:

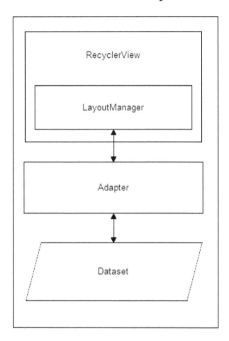

To add the layout manager, open your main activity Java file and include the following two fields:

```
private Toolbar toolbar;
privateRecyclerViewrecyclerView;
```

In the `onCreate()` method, add the following lines:

```
recyclerView = (RecyclerView) findViewById(R.id.list);
recyclerView.setHasFixedSize(true);

RecyclerView.LayoutManagerlayoutManager = new
LinearLayoutManager(this);
recyclerView.setLayoutManager(layoutManager);
```

```
ArrayList<Contact> contacts = new ArrayList<Contact>();

RecyclerView.Adapter adapter = new RecyclerViewAdapter(contacts);
recyclerView.setAdapter(adapter);
```

This is all we do to set up the LayoutManager, but the Adapter class needs to be created more or less from scratch. Create a new public Java class called `RecyclerViewAdapter.java` and ensure that it extends `RecyclerView.Adapter<RecyclerViewAdapter.ContactViewHolder>`. This will generate an error; click on the red quick-fix icon and implement the methods suggested.

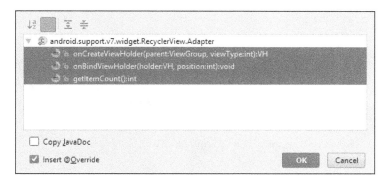

These three methods, once filled out, will look like the following:

```
@Override
publicContactViewHolderonCreateViewHolder(ViewGroup parent,
intviewType) {
    View v = LayoutInflater.from(parent.getContext()).inflate(R.
layout.card_layout, parent, false);
ContactViewHoldercontactViewHolder = new ContactViewHolder(v);
returncontactViewHolder;
}

@Override
public void onBindViewHolder(ContactViewHolder holder, int position) {
holder.profilePic.setImageResource(contacts.get(position).profilePic);
holder.name.setText(contacts.get(position).name);
holder.status.setText(contacts.get(position).status);
}

@Override
publicintgetItemCount() {
returncontacts.size();
}
```

You will also need to add the `onAttachedToRecyclerView()` method, like so:

```
@Override
public void onAttachedToRecyclerView(RecyclerViewrecyclerView) {
super.onAttachedToRecyclerView(recyclerView);
}
```

And finally, ViewHolder:

```
public static class ContactViewHolder extends RecyclerView.ViewHolder
{
CardViewcardView;
ImageViewprofilePic;
TextView name;
TextView status;

publicContactViewHolder(View itemView) {
super(itemView);
cardView = (CardView) itemView.findViewById(R.id.card_view);
profilePic = (ImageView) itemView.findViewById(R.id.profile_pic);
name = (TextView) itemView.findViewById(R.id.name);
status = (TextView) itemView.findViewById(R.id.status);
    }
}
```

The ViewHolder pattern is the final part of our data jigsaw. It speeds up long lists by only making one call to `findViewById()`, which is a resource-hungry process.

The example can now be run on an emulator or handset, and will have an output similar to that seen here:

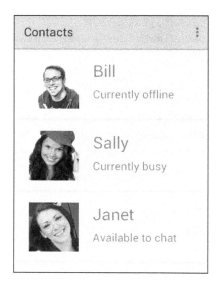

The example we have worked through here explains enough of how RecyclerView works to be able to implement one in a variety of situations. We used a LinearLayoutManager here to create our list, but there is also GridLayoutManager and StaggeredGridLayoutManager that work in a very similar fashion.

The CardView, on the other hand, is used in a wide variety of different application settings, and from a Material Design perspective, there is a lot more to cover.

Cards

CardView is probably the most frequently used and flexible material component, and as such, there are a considerable number of guidelines concerning its structure, appearance, and function. Cards are described by Google as being entry points to more detailed information. This means that they should provide a small number of actions in the form of buttons, clickable images, and often, simply the card itself.

The way we used cards in the previous section, to create a list, is probably not the best example of how to employ CardView. Generally, with lists of items with very similar content, a simple divider provides a far less cluttered layout, and cards were used here just to demonstrate RecyclerViews in an easily digestible fashion.

Cards come into their own when they can be be presented in a collection where they do not all share identical layouts. In fact, one of the things that makes cards so useful is that although they are required to have uniform widths, there is no necessity for them to share their heights, format, content, or color.

The preceding CardView is a good example of how blocks of content can be structured. It is explained as follows:

- The Header at the top is optional; it contains an avatar, a title, and a subtitle
- It should be 72 dp high and have 16 dp padding all round, meaning that the avatar should have a diameter of 40 dp
- The title is 14 sp or 24 sp when there is no avatar
- The subtitle is 14 sp and uses your secondary text transparency
- The image has a 16:9 aspect ratio, although 1:1 is also allowed
- The supporting text is 14 sp and has padding of 24 dp at the bottom and 16 dp on the other sides
- Actions are all caps 16sp, and should use your accent color or another color with strong emphasis

Cards are a very dynamic component, able to be moved, rearranged, and dismissed. The elevation for a card at rest is 2 dp, and 8 dp when selected and moving, although if your cards are contained in a CoordinatorLayout, this will be handled automatically.

Tiles

Despite CardView's versatility, it is not always the best solution. Its ideal use is to display content that cannot be formatted identically in every instance. When content is homogeneous across an entire collection, such as in a photo gallery, then a cleaner, simpler layout can be created using tiles rather than cards. For example, take a look at the following image:

As can be seen in the example, tiles do not have rounded corners or shadows, but provide a very clean interface for items that each have a single action and identical layout format.

There is no specific widget or view for tiles, and they can be constructed with ImageViews, TextViews, or whatever else suits our purposes.

Summary

Representing data in lists and grids is a powerful technique that makes up a large part of many applications, and the layouts and views provided by the design and support libraries allow us to create the clean and simple layouts associated with Material Design.

CardView lies at the heart of many successful material layouts, and is one of the most useful and recognizable material views, allowing us to present content in an intuitive manner.

One of the things Material Design is best known for is animation. Not only does does this make our apps look fantastic, but can also be very functional and instructional, giving the user a clearer sense of application flow and purpose, and this is what we will be tackling in the next chapter.

6
Animations and Transitions

Of all of Material Design's features, animation is probably the most important and exciting. Not only does it allow for the creation of beautiful, dynamic, and fun interfaces, but animation can also serve a useful purpose instructing and directing the user in a visual rather than written fashion. For example, when a user swipes a component and it disappears from the screen, it is obvious that the item has been dismissed. Likewise, when a component is tapped and it expands to provide more detail, there is no need to explain its functionality as this is visually apparent.

The vast majority of the time, the default material animations are perfectly suited to our purposes and are very easy to implement, particularly when using the CoordinatorLayout provided by the design support library. However, it is possible, and often desirable, to generate custom animations. Not only is this a lot of fun, it is also a great way to learn the material guidelines regarding motion.

In this chapter, we will learn how to:

- Understand touch feedback
- Generate ripple animations
- Hide and reveal elements
- Create logical transitions
- Manage entrances and exits
- Animate shared components across activities
- Understand motion and material physics

Touch feedback

One of the primary objectives of Material Design is to create a tactile experience for the user. It is essential to inform the user instantly, whenever they interact with any active component. This can be done in a variety of ways, such as increasing the elevation of a view upon contact, but the most common and stylish way is the ripple effect animation, which, as its name suggests, sends a ripple of color across a view, layout, or screen, emanating from the point of contact.

Ripple animations

The ripple animation effect is one of the most widely recognized material animations and provides a great example of what Google refers to as responsive interaction. Ripples are applied automatically to clickable widgets such as buttons, but there are many situations where they would be perfectly applied to other views, such as image and text views, or even entire layouts.

Fortunately, adding the ripple touch response to other views and screen components is remarkably simple. The following XML definition demonstrates just how to add the ripple effect to any view:

```
<TextView
android:id="@+id/text_view"
    android:layout_width="wrap_content"
    android:layout_height="wrap_content"
android:background="?android:attr/selectableItemBackground"
android:clickable="true"

    android:text="@string/ripple_example" />
```

The two highlighted lines in this snippet allow us to include this effect very simply on almost any view we choose. Trying this out, you will see that the ripple effect stops at the border of the view we applied it to. We can extend the effect though, by changing the `android:background` attribute as follows:

```
"?android:attr/selectableItemBackgroundBorderless"
```

This will have the effect of allowing the ripple to continue beyond the border of its defining view until it reaches the borders of its parent container. This provides us with the ability to control the emphasis that a particular action has. A ripple that spreads only across a particular widget explains to the user that that widget has been activated, but a ripple that fills a whole card or screen immediately informs the user that the action has a wider affect and that a more significant transition is taking place.

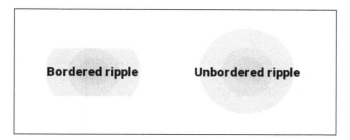

It is very handy to be able to apply the ripple effect to any view of our choice, but there is more we can do if we drill down a little and create our own ripple animation from scratch.

A ripple animation can be created in XML very simply, using the `RippleDrawable` class. Open the `res/drawable` folder and create a new XML file called something along the lines of `ripple.xml`. The very least it requires to work is the following code:

```
<?xml version="1.0" encoding="utf-8"?>
<ripple xmlns:android="http://schemas.android.com/apk/res/android"
android:color="?android:colorControlHighlight">
</ripple>
```

It can then be associated with a view of our choice in a very similar manner to the previous example. Simply set the `background` property as shown next:

```
android:background="@drawable/ripple"
```

There is a lot more that can be done now that we have direct control over the animation. For example, if you have tested the previous code, you will have noticed that it produces a borderless ripple. With XML, we can create our own border very simply with a mask.

Masks are defined mainly by their shape. This can be `rectangle`, `round`, `oval`, and `ring`, depending on the shape of the view or view group that we wish to bind our ripple within, which is usually `rectangle`. The example here creates a bounded rectangle animation, and sets the color of the ripple to our accent color, as defined in our material theme:

```xml
<?xml version="1.0" encoding="utf-8"?>
<ripple xmlns:android="http://schemas.android.com/apk/res/android"
android:color="?android:colorControlHighlight">

<item android:id="@android:id/mask">
<shape android:shape="rectangle">
<solid android:color="?android:colorAccent" />
</shape>
</item>

</ripple>
```

The preceding code is almost self explanatory, but it is important to note that the ID value must be `mask`, and the use of solid in the color definition has alternative settings, not all of which will work for every animation. To see and experiment with these options, select the value and press *Ctrl + Space*.

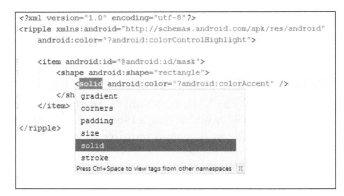

 Pressing *Ctrl + Space* can be used across Android Studio to examine available options.

It is all very well to know how to acknowledge user input, but of course, we need to respond to these interactions. Very often, the most useful application of material animation is to take the user from one activity to another in a meaningful and logical fashion, but before we get to these transitions, we need to cover situations where the user remains within the same activity, but their actions reveal or hide components within it.

Revealing and hiding

Placing views and view groups in a layout and setting them as invisible, to be revealed later, is a lightweight and useful technique for changing the appearance of a screen without having to load separate activities or fragments. Furthermore, the circular reveal is designed specifically with material in mind.

Any view can be hidden and revealed, but for the sake of this exercise, we will use the following `ImageView` XML definition:

```
<ImageView
android:id="@+id/image_view"
android:layout_width="wrap_content"
android:layout_height="wrap_content"
android:layout_alignParentTop="true"
android:layout_centerHorizontal="true"
android:src="@drawable/some_image"
android:visibility="invisible" />
```

Reveal animations can be triggered by almost any event, but here we will simply use a button press. In your Java activity file, declare the button and image views as fields:

```
private ImageView imageView;
private Buttton button;
```

These need to be associated with their XML counterparts in the `onCreate()` method:

```
imageView = (ImageView) findViewById(R.id.image_view);
button = (Button) findViewById(R.id.button);
```

Next, we need to set up a click listener, which can be done by changing the class declaration so that it implements `View.OnClickListener`, as shown next:

```
public class MainActivity extends Activity implements View.
OnClickListener
```

This will require that you then implement the `onClick()` method. This is where we will place our code to trigger the animation. When you are finished, it will look like this:

```
@Override
public void onClick(View v) {
int x = imageView.getWidth() / 2;
int y = imageView.getHeight() / 2;
int endRadius = Math.max(imageView.getWidth(), imageView.getHeight());
```

```
Animator circularReveal = ViewAnimationUtils.
createCircularReveal(imageView, x, y, 0, endRadius);
imageView.setVisibility(View.VISIBLE);
circularReveal.start();
}
```

Reversing the direction of the animation and causing the view to become invisible again is a tiny bit more complex. Firstly, we need to calculate the start radius rather than the end one, and secondly, we need an animation listener to detect when the animation is complete so that we can make the view invisible again. The code should look like this:

```
int x = imageView.getWidth() / 2;
int y = imageView.getHeight() / 2;
int startRadius = imageView.getWidth();
Animator circularReveal = ViewAnimationUtils.
createCircularReveal(imageView, x, y, startRadius, 0);

circularReveal.addListener(new AnimatorListenerAdapter() {
@Override
public void onAnimationEnd(Animator anim) {
super.onAnimationEnd(anim);
imageView.setVisibility(View.INVISIBLE);
}
});

circularReveal.start();
```

The circular reveal animation provides an elegant and efficient way to create and destroy material dynamically. It can be applied to any view, and also view groups, although it has to be borne in mind that it is best suited for creating a single sheet of material rather than a complex layout.

Many applications, if not most, contain more than one activity, and one of the most important uses of animation in Material Design is to inform the user of these transitions.

Transitions

Android versions with an API level of 21 or higher come with a set of material-design-compliant transition animations. As one would imagine, transition animations give us control over how components exit a screen and how they enter. This is all made possible with the **TransitionManager**.

Exits and entrances

The best introduction to the TransitionManager is to see it in action. This can be achieved with a simple example, where we get to see the types of animation available to us before tackling the mechanics of actually moving from one activity to another. This will also give us the opportunity to take a quick look at the GridLayout, which we have not yet covered:

1. Start a new Android project with an API level of 21 or higher.

2. Inside the root layout, add a GridLayout.

3. You will need to include the ID, `rowCount`, and `columnCount` attributes in the layout definition, as highlighted next:

```
<GridLayout xmlns:android="http://schemas.android.com/apk/res/
android"
xmlns:tools="http://schemas.android.com/tools"
android:id="@+id/view_group"
    android:layout_width="match_parent"
    android:layout_height="match_parent"
android:columnCount="2"
android:rowCount="2"
  tools:context=".MainActivity">
```

4. This example demonstrates a 2 x 2 grid, but you could, of course, have more if you so chose.

5. Find or create some images and put together a simple layout like the one seen next:

6. Provide IDs for each image, using a naming convention along the lines of the one seen here:

```
<ImageView
android:id="@+id/image_01"
android:layout_column="0"
    android:layout_row="0"
    android:clickable="true"
    android:src="@drawable/image_01" />
```

7. In the steps, GridLayout, include a button.

8. Open your activity Java file and declare it so that it implements a click listener, as we did in the previous example:

```
public class MainActivity extends Activity implements View.
OnClickListener
```

9. Create fields for the GridLayout and your images:

```
private ViewGroup viewGroup;
private ImageView image_01, image_02, image_03, image_04;
```

10. Associate these views with their XML counterparts in the onCreate() method:

```
viewGroup = (ViewGroup)findViewById(R.id.view_group);
image_01 = (ImageView)findViewById(R.id.image_01);
image_02 = (ImageView)findViewById(R.id.image_02);
image_03 = (ImageView)findViewById(R.id.image_03);
image_04 = (ImageView)findViewById(R.id.image_04);
```

11. Complete the onClick() method, as shown here:

```
@Override
public void onClick(View v) {
TransitionManager.beginDelayedTransition(viewGroup, new
Explode());
    toggle(image_01, image_02, image_03, image_04);
}
```

12. Finally, add the toggle() method:

```
private static void toggle(View... views) {
for (View v : views) {
boolean isVisible = v.getVisibility() == View.VISIBLE;
        v.setVisibility(isVisible ? View.INVISIBLE : View.
VISIBLE);
    }
}
```

You can now compile and run the project to see the effect of the explode transition. As you would imagine, explode is not the only transition available to us. To see how these work, simply replace `Explode()` in the `onClick()` method with any of the following:

- `Slide()`
- `Fade()`
- `AutoTransition()`

Slide and fade should require no explanation, however, **AutoTransition** might. What it does is fade out non-shared components, then move and resize shared elements, and finally fade in new views and widgets, and this is very often the ideal solution for material layouts.

As you try out the preceding alternative animations, you may notice that the editor fails to recognize them. This is most likely due to the classes having not been imported. Although it can often be rectified by pressing *Alt + Enter*, there is a far simpler way to organize your imports. From the **File** menu, navigate to **Settings | Editor | General | Auto Import** and check the boxes, as shown here:

The previous example is not strictly speaking a transition, as all the animations take place within a single activity, but it is a good way to explore the animations themselves. Once we move on to see how switching between two or more activities is achieved, we also get to see one of the coolest features of material animation, which involves how transitions work when a component is shared across both exiting and entering activities.

Shared components

Very often, when an app transitions from one activity to another, there will be elements that appear in both. For example, a user might select a thumbnail image from a grid with the intention of viewing a larger version of the image, and this image would be considered a shared element. In this example, we would want the other images to slide, fade, or explode out of sight, but we would not want our selected image to disappear and then reappear, as this would involve unnecessary movement and could even be considered confusing. Ideally, what we are after is for our shared element to move and grow smoothly from its original position to its resting place in the opened activity.

Programming this kind of behavior is fortunately quite simple. At its very simplest, all we need to do is enable transition animations in our theme, and this will produce the default fade transition whenever a user navigates from one activity to another. More excitingly, we can define our own transitions for entries and exits, as well as shared components.

To enable transitions in your application, simply include the following item in your custom style definition:

```
<item name="android:windowContentTransitions">true</item>
```

To create a custom transition, you will need to create a new folder in the `res` directory called `transition`. You can then create XML files to define each of your transitions. More than likely, you will have one for entering shared components, one for exiting shared objects, as well as an entering and exiting transition for other elements, and if your app contains a wide variety of components, you may have a lot more.

If you are thinking that this sounds like a lot of work, it is well worth bearing in mind that the default implementation of transition animations is set up with Material Design in mind, and probably is all you will ever need.

XML transitions are defined with the `transitionSet` tag. These can be quite complex and contain long strings of behavior, but they can also be very simple. For example, creating a file such as `res/transition/some_transition.xml`, and completing it as shown next, would be sufficient to re-size a view:

```
<transitionSet xmlns:android="http://schemas.android.com/apk/res/
android">
<changeBounds/>
</transitionSet>
```

This example contains only one element, but `transitionSets` can contain many, and following is a list of other elements we can include:

```
<changeBounds/>
<changeClipBounds/>
<changeImageTransform/>
<autoTransition/>
<explode/>
<fade/>
<slide/>
```

The best way to see how these work is to try them out, although it is worth knowing now that `changeImageTransform` will scale and rotate images when necessary.

When we choose to apply more than one effect, we can also decide if we want our animations to be applied simultaneously or sequentially by editing the `transitionSet` tag to the following:

```
<transitionSet xmlns:android="http://schemas.android.com/apk/res/
android"
android:transitionOrdering="sequential">
```

Or, we can also do this:

```
<transitionSet xmlns:android="http://schemas.android.com/apk/res/
android"
android:transitionOrdering="together">
```

From a material perspective, sequential ordering is preferred, as having too many things happen at once can reduce the clarity of the transition, but bearing that in mind, there are many elegant and logical simultaneous material transitions.

We can also target a specific view or view group in our transitions; the following example brings these features of custom transitions together:

```
<transitionSet xmlns:android="http://schemas.android.com/apk/res/
android"
android:transitionOrdering="together">
<slide/>
<fade android:fadingMode="fade_in" >
<targets>
<target android:targetId="@id/some_view" />
</targets>
</fade>
</transitionSet>
```

Once we have defined a transition like this, we can apply it to our app via our style definition, as shown next:

```
<item name="android:windowEnterTransition">@transition/my_entrance_
transition</item>
<item name="android:windowExitTransition">@transition/my_exit_
transition</item>
```

For shared element transitions, use the following:

```
<item name="android:windowSharedElementEnterTransition">@transition/
my_image_transition</item>
<item name="android:windowSharedElementExitTransition">@transition/
my_image_transition</item>
```

Of course, once this is done, we will need a project with more than one activity. This will involve at least two Java activity classes and an XML layout for each. To test out our transitions, the activities do not need to do very much; a single button or clickable view will be enough to start a new activity. This can be achieved with a single line, most usually within an `onClick()` method:

```
startActivity(intent, ActivityOptions.makeSceneTransitionAnimation(th
is).toBundle());
```

When this code is called, and there is an exit transition defined for the activity, then this animation will be triggered. Note that if there is also an entry transition defined for the incoming activity, then this too will be called.

Finally, we need a way to inform the system which elements are shared, and this is done by providing the corresponding elements in each activity with a common name. This is done with the `transitionName` attribute, as shown next:

```
<ImageView
android:id="@+id/some_image"
android:transitionName="shared_name"
android:src="@drawable/shared_image" />
```

The SDK provides many powerful tools for animation, and one could easily write an entire book on the subject. From a material point of view, we are fortunate that we can rely on the default settings and provided transitions to generate the kinds of motion that are so important to the Material Design experience. Whether we intend to stick to the default implementations or explore custom animations further, there are some specific material guidelines regarding what Google refers to as authentic motion.

Realistic movement

As mentioned at the beginning of the book, material needs to be thought of as sharing many of the properties found in real-world objects, such as existing in a three-dimensional space and casting shadows. Nowhere are the physical properties of material more important than when it is in motion.

Material should be thought of as having its own laws of physics, and although no knowledge of actual physics is required, a general understanding of how everyday objects behave is probably the best way to understand authentic motion.

Material should be thought of as having mass and being subject to friction. Real world objects cannot go from stationary to moving at a particular speed instantaneously. They must first overcome their own inertia so as to accelerate, which in turn generates momentum. Similarly, they cannot stop then without resisting that momentum. By mimicking these behaviors, material provides a virtual environment that feels almost tangible, and certainly recognizable to the user.

Think of the cartoons we watched as children; quite often a character would run over the edge of a precipice and continue running until they realized their error. Now, despite the ridiculousness of the idea, this illusion was maintained by very carefully thought out motion and timing. Had the character suddenly fallen downward, which does not coincide with the way we experience everyday objects falling, the illusion would been utterly destroyed and the humor lost.

Although far from easy to explain, the manner in which solid objects accelerate and decelerate is something the human mind is keyed into. We understand intuitively that heavy objects take longer to accelerate and slow down than light objects.

The acceleration/deceleration process is by no means symmetrical; entry and exit transitions are not simply mirrors of each other. Acceleration is an accumulative process, the faster you are going, the faster you can go, and deceleration is the reverse, rather than the mirror of it.

Most times, we will never have to worry about this, but authentic motion is a significant part of material animation, and when generating animations from scratch, realistic movement can make all the difference.

Summary

Animation is probably material's most distinguishing feature, and it allows us to create beautiful and dynamic applications that engage and delight the user. As Material Design has grown, animating apps has become considerably easier, and many of the guidelines are now baked into the SDK. It is the simplicity and naturalness of these animations that make Material Design a language that will be around for a very long time.

In this chapter, we saw how to use motion to respond to user interaction, and how to take the user from one activity to another in a seamless and intuitive fashion. Using philosophies taken from traditional animation gives material applications a physical and natural feel.

Having covered layouts, data management, common material components, and motion, we can now take a look at implementing material on a wider variety of devices, which is a journey we will begin in the next chapter.

Material on Other Devices

7

So far, this book has been primarily concerned with material for handheld devices such as phones and tablets. This is largely due to the fact that Android Studio is purpose built and comes with a myriad of material tools, making it ideal for learning Material Design principles.

Of course, material is far from limited to these devices, or even Google devices, and is now appearing on a growing number of platforms including an increasing number of iOS applications.

Having mastered the fundamentals of Material Design, we can now take a look at how it is applied across a wide variety of form factors, ranging from the minute screens of wearables, right up to the 10 feet of many TV devices.

In this chapter, you will learn how to:

- Run the TV project template
- Include an application banner to the home screen
- Apply manifest permissions and feature uses
- Implement the Leanback Support Library
- Understand TV application structure
- Create a recommendation card
- Pair a wearable device with a handset
- Manage different Wearable screen shapes
- Create Wearable layouts

After mobile devices, material is found most often on our desktops, as web pages and stand alone applications. There are some interesting differences between mobile and desktop material, and these require a different set of tools such as MDL, which we will examine in detail later in the book. For now, we will see how material can be applied to other Google and Android devices, starting with Android TV.

Material TV

Televisions offer an exciting challenge for developers and designers alike. Most large screens are designed to be viewed from up to 10 feet away, and the controls differ from the touchscreens that we are used to dealing with. The interface too is very different, with the toolbar being replaced by a sidebar index or browse lane, and the content being represented in rows of categories. These two elements move in tandem with each other; the lane slides upward as each row is highlighted as shown in the following image:

Most Android TV apps take advantage of the Leanback Library, which provides numerous widgets specifically designed for TV, along with the Leanback theme, which is a TV-optimized version of the material theme.

 The Leanback Library is a v17 library, which means it will only work with API levels of 17 (Android 4.2.2) or higher.

The sheer size of today's televisions allows us to represent our apps graphically with far more than a simple icon, and TV apps allow a 320 x 180 dp space called a **banner** for each app on the home screen.

Banners

The home screen is the entry point for Android TV users. From here, they can search for content, adjust settings, and access applications and games. In the first view the user will get of our app will be on this screen in the form of a banner image. This is what they will use to launch the app.

Every TV app has a banner image. This is a 320 x 180 dp bitmap that should portray what our app does in a simple and efficient manner. For example:

Banners can contain colorful photographic imagery too, but text should always be kept bold and to a minimum. The banner can then be declared in the project manifest. To see how this is done, and how other manifest properties relevant to TV apps can be set, follow these steps:

1. Start a new project, selecting **TV** as **Target Android Device** and **Android TV Activity** as the **activity template**.

2. Add your image to the `drawable` folder and call it `banner` or something like that.

3. Open the `manifests/AndroidManifest.xml` file.

4. Delete the following line:

    ```
    android:banner="@drawable/app_icon_your_company"
    ```

5. Edit the opening `<application>` node to include the following highlighted line:

    ```
    <application
        android:allowBackup="true"
    android:banner="@drawable/banner"
        android:label="@string/app_name"
        android:supportsRtl="true"
        android:theme="@style/Theme.Leanback">
    ```

6. In the root `<manifest>` node, add the following attribute:

```
<uses-feature
    android:name="android.hardware.microphone"
    android:required="false" />
```

This last `<uses-feature>` node is not strictly required, but will make your app available to older televisions that do not have microphones included. If your app relies on voice control, then omit this attribute.

If you are building for TV alone, then this is all you need to do in terms of making your app available in the TV section of the Play Store. However, you may be developing an application such as a game that can be played on other devices. In this case, also include the following clause to make it available to devices that can be rotated:

```
<uses-feature
android:name="android.hardware.screen.portrait"
android:required="false" />
```

In these situations, you should also set `"android.software.leanback"` to `required="false"`, and revert to the material or AppCompat themes.

You may be wondering why we moved the banner declaration from the main activity to the application as a whole. This was not strictly necessary, and what we have done is simply apply one banner to the whole app, regardless of how many activities it contains. Unless you want separate banners for each activity, this is usually the best way to go.

If you are not starting your project from the template, you will need to implement `Theme.Leanback` yourself, and include this dependency in your `build.gradle` file:

```
compile 'com.android.support:leanback-v17:23.0.1'
```

If you have taken a look around the TV template code, you will have realized that there is a lot to coding an Android TV application; far more than can be covered here. Examining the template code yields some valuable clues as to how TV apps are put together.

TV app structure

A large number of TV apps offer a limited set of functions, and this is usually all that is required. For the most part, users want to:

* Browse for content
* Search for content
* Consume content

The Leanback Library provides fragment classes for each of these. A typical browse view is provided by `BrowserFragment` and the template demonstrates this with a simple example, along with `SearchFragment`.

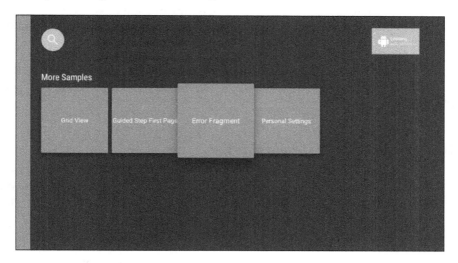

The consumption view is provided by `PlaybackOverlayFragment`, and is probably the simplest of views comprising of little more than a VideoView and the controls.

There is also `DetailsFragment` that provides content-specific information. The content and layout of this view are dependent on the subject matter and can take any form you choose, with the regular rules of Material Design applying. The design view scrolls up from the bottom of the consumption view.

The Leanback Library makes light work of bringing Material Design to TV devices. If you decide to use views from elsewhere, then the same material rules that apply to them elsewhere, will apply here too. Before moving on to other form factors, it is worth mentioning that background images need to have a 5 percent bleed around the edges to ensure they reach the sides of all TV screens. This means that a 1280 x 720 px image needs to be 1408 x 792 px.

Despite the Leanback Library taking care of all our Material Design considerations, there is one situation where we need to be aware of the guidelines, and that is the recommendation card.

Recommendation cards

The top row of the Android TV home screen is the recommendation row. This allows the user to quickly access content based on their viewing history. Content can be recommended because it is a continuation of previously viewed content, or related in some way based on the user's viewing history.

When designing recommendation cards, there are only a handful of design factors we need to consider. These cards are constructed from an image or large icon, a title, a subtitle, and application icon, as shown as follows:

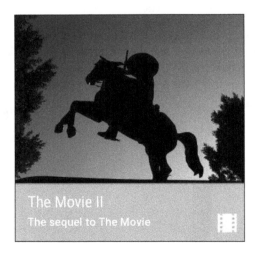

There is a certain amount of flexibility when it comes to the aspect ratio of the card image. The width of the card must never be less than two-third of its height or more than one and a half. There must be no transparent elements within the image and it must not be less than 176 dp in height.

Large expanses of white can be quite harsh on many televisions. If you need large areas of white, use #EEE rather than #FFF.

If you take a look at the recommendation row on a live Android TV set, you will see that, as each card is highlighted, the background image changes, and we too should provide a background image as well for each recommendation card. These images must differ from the one on the card and be 2016 x 1134 px to allow for a 5 percent bleed, and ensure that they leave no gaps around the edge of the screen. These images too should have no transparent sections.

There is a great deal to programming recommendations and unfortunately too much to cover here. There is, however, a very useful guide in the official documentation, which can be found at http://developer.android.com/training/tv/discovery/recommendations.html.

The challenge of designing for such large screens affords us the opportunity to include colorful and vibrant imagery with high-quality graphics. At the other end of this size spectrum falls the wearable device, where space is at a premium and a totally different approach is required when applying Material Design.

Wearable material

Whereas TV apps are almost exclusively for finding and consuming video content, Wearable apps can, and do, perform a huge number of functions, and for this reason are more like handheld apps. Although heavily dependent on the card, almost any widget can be used in an Android Wear application, and just as with handheld applications, there are a series of specific rules governing the sizes, margins, and positioning of screen components.

Unlike most devices that operate independently, Wearable Android devices need to be coupled with a handset that does most of the processing, and before we can explore material layouts, we need to see how this pairing is achieved at a technical level.

Connecting to a Wearable device

It is not necessary to have access to a physical Wearable device to develop and design apps for Wear, as this can be done with an emulator created with the AVD manager. If you have not already done so, ensure that you have downloaded the appropriate system image for the API platform you are intending to design for, as demonstrated in the following image taken from the SDK Manager:

As you will know, Android Wear devices are available with both round and square faces. There are two distinct approaches to managing this distinction, and to see how this is done best, it is a good idea to create two emulators, one for each format.

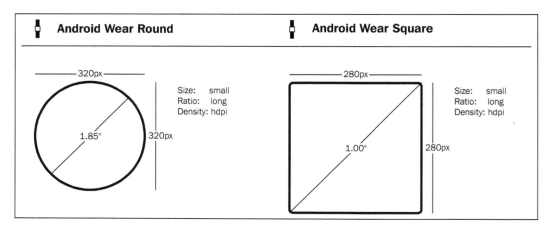

There is also a chinned version available, but for testing purposes, this can be considered the same as the round version.

How you pair the wearable AVD will depend on whether you are coupling it with a real handset or another emulator. If you are using a handset, you will need to download the Android Wear app from `https://play.google.com/store/apps/details?id=com.google.android.wearable.app`.

Then locate the `adb.exe` file, which is probably located somewhere around `user\AppData\Local\Android\sdk\platform-tools\`.

Open the command window here and issue the following command:

`adb -d forward tcp:5601 tcp:5601.`

You can now launch the companion app and follow the instructions to pair the devices.

 You will need to issue this port-forwarding command each time you connect the handset.

If you are pairing your wearable emulator with an emulated handset, then you will need an AVD that targets Google APIs rather than a regular Android platform. You can then download `com.google.android.wearable.app-2.apk`. There are many places online where this can be found. I used `http://www.apkmirror.com/apk/google-inc/android-wear/android-wear-1-3-0-2223019-android-apk-download/`. The APK should be placed in your `sdk/platform-tools` directory, where it can be installed with the following command:

`adb install com.google.android.wearable.app-2.apk`

Now, start your Wearable AVD and enter `adb` devices into the command prompt, making sure that both emulators are visible with an output similar to this:

```
List of devices attached
emulator-5554    device
emulator-5555    device
```

Enter `adb telnet localhost 5554` at the command prompt, where `5554` is the phone emulator. Next, enter `adb redir add tcp:5601:5601`. You can now use the Wear app on the handheld AVD to connect to the watch.

When creating an Android Wear project, you will need to include two modules: one for the Wearable component and one for the handset by check both boxes in the project window as seen in this screenshot:

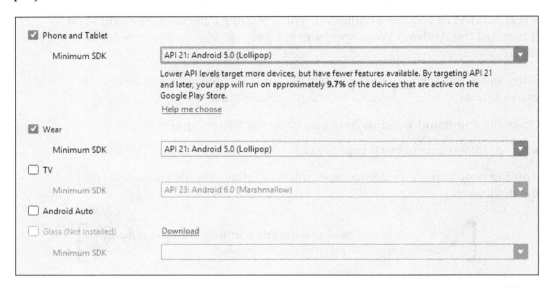

Android provides a Wearable UI Support Library that provides some very useful features for Wear developers and designers. If you have created a Wearable project using the wizard, this will have been included during setup. Otherwise, you will need to include the following dependencies in the module: `wearbuild.gradle` file:

```
compile 'com.google.android.support:wearable:1.3.0'
compile 'com.google.android.gms:play-services-wearable:8.1.0'
```

You will also require these dependencies in the module: `mobile build` file:

```
wearApp project(':wear')
compile 'com.google.android.gms:play-services:8.1.0'
```

Note that these libraries will, no doubt, have been updated by the time you read this, and you will need to check using the SDK Manager for the latest version.

Version numbers can be replaced with a + symbol, for example: `com.google.android.gms:play-services:+`. This is supposed to compile the latest version but cannot be guaranteed to work on all future versions.

Managing differently shaped screens

Android Wearable devices come in two basic shapes: square and round. There is a chinned round version but this can be considered the same as the round screen from a design point of view.

In advance, we have no idea which of these shapes our apps will be running on, and there are two solutions to this conundrum. The first, and most obvious, is to simply create a layout for each shape, and this is very often the best solution. If you have a Wearable project created with the wizard, and you open the `res/layout` folder in the Wear module, you will see that template activities for both shapes have been included.

We still need a way to detect the screen shape when the app is run on an actual device or emulator so that it knows which layout to inflate. This is done with `WatchViewStub,` and the code to call it has to be included in the `onCreate()` method of the main Java activity file, as shown as follows:

```
@Override
protected void onCreate(Bundle savedInstanceState) {
super.onCreate(savedInstanceState);
setContentView(R.layout.activity_main);
final WatchViewStub stub = (WatchViewStub) findViewById(R.id.watch_
view_stub);
stub.setOnLayoutInflatedListener(new WatchViewStub.
OnLayoutInflatedListener() {
@Override
public void onLayoutInflated(WatchViewStub stub) {
mTextView = (TextView) stub.findViewById(R.id.text);
}
});
}
```

This can then be implemented in XML like this:

```
<android.support.wearable.view.WatchViewStub xmlns:android="http://
schemas.android.com/apk/res/android"
xmlns:app="http://schemas.android.com/apk/res-auto"
xmlns:tools="http://schemas.android.com/tools"
android:id="@+id/watch_view_stub"
android:layout_width="match_parent"
android:layout_height="match_parent"
app:rectLayout="@layout/rect_activity_main"
app:roundLayout="@layout/round_activity_main"
tools:context=".MainActivity"
tools:deviceIds="wear"></android.support.wearable.view.WatchViewStub>
```

The alternative to creating separate layouts for each screen shape is to use a layout that itself is aware of the screen shape. This comes in the form of BoxInsetLayout, which adjusts padding settings for round screens and only positions views within the highlighted square, as seen in the following screenshot:

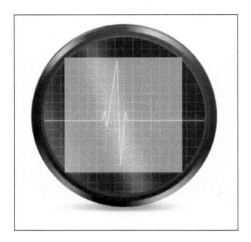

BoxInsetLayout can be used, like any other layout, as the root ViewGroup in your main XML activity:

```
<android.support.wearable.view.BoxInsetLayout
xmlns:android="http://schemas.android.com/apk/res/android"
xmlns:app="http://schemas.android.com/apk/res-auto"
android:layout_height="match_parent"
android:layout_width="match_parent"
android:padding="15dp">

    .   .   .


</android.support.wearable.view.BoxInsetLayout>
```

The padding of 15 dp is only applied to square screens, as 15 dp is also the margin width and height that the round screen exhibits at its widest points, and 15 dp is always subtracted from any padding we set for the root view on a round screen.

The convenience of BoxInsetLayout is offset by its lack of flexibility, and as we are material designers, it is always preferable to maintain complete control over settings such as margins and padding, and for this reason, we should generally opt for the distinct layout option.

Whichever of the previously mentioned methods we adopt, we will no doubt want to create custom layouts of our own, and these will inevitably utilize the card view.

Wearable layouts

Nearly all content in an Android Wear app is presented using the CardView. There are strict guidelines regarding the size, text, and positioning of the cards. At its simplest, a card will contain a title, an app icon, and a single line of text.

The rules for this card are as follows:

- The card has an 8 dp margin around its bottom and sides
- It cannot be shorter than 72 dp
- The icon is 32 x 32 dp and is inset 8 dp from the right-hand side edge
- The baseline of the content text is 16 dp from the bottom of the card
- The text is indented by 16 dp and cannot extend closer than 16 dp to the right-hand side edge
- Each line of text is 28 dp tall
- The font for both lines is Roboto Condensed Light 20 sp
- The text color of the title is #A2A2A2
- The content text color is #434343

The same principles can be applied to two-line content messages, with the card being 96 dp high. This is the highest a card can be on Wear, and if you have more lines of text, then the card needs to be scrollable with the extra text underneath the screen. Generally speaking, lengthy text is to be avoided on Wearable devices, and the principles here can be used to construct most of the cards we will need. There is, however, a handy toolkit that can be downloaded from http://developer.android.com/design/downloads/index.html.

Wearables represent a powerful opportunity for developers, and a clear, well thought out design can make all the difference to an app that, more often than not, will rarely receive more than a quick glance.

Summary

Designing for the very small and the very large brings interesting challenges for developers and designers alike. In both cases, Material Design allows us to create attractive and easy-to-understand interfaces. This is especially the case with Wearables, where the interface will most likely be a companion app to one running on a handset, and material provides a great shared medium for both.

After phones and tablets, it is the desktop that has seen the largest uptake of Material Design, and although it is perfectly possible to take what we have learned and create Material Designs using conventional web technology, there are some very useful tools that are available to us. The remaining chapters of this book cover the technologies that are most frequently used and easily mastered when it comes to creating material web pages and apps; namely CSS frameworks, which have many of the features of Material Design built into them.

8

Material Web Frameworks

Developing and designing for desktop environments differs in many ways from mobile environments. There is the larger screen, the absence of a touchscreen, and most significantly, a large number of browsers and operating systems that our page or app may find itself running on.

Although Android Studio and SDK are really the only choice when it comes to developing Android apps, there are a lot of options when it comes to web design. By far the fastest way to develop is with a CSS framework. This generally provides the CSS and JavaScript files that make up an empty web project. Which of these frameworks we use depends on several factors, including the purpose of our project and previous experience.

In this chapter, we will take an introductory look at two of the most commonly used frameworks, **Materialize** and **Material Design Lite** (**MDL**). We will also briefly cover some of the other tools available, and these will demonstrate the different approach required when implementing Material Design on the Web.

In this chapter, we will cover the following topics:

- Explore desktop layout structure
- Install the Bower package manager
- Materialize
- Download and set up Materialize
- Add a navigation bar
- Apply elevation and shadow
- Apply a material color theme
- Layout an adaptive page
- Include and layout cards

- Customize buttons
- Apply material icons
- MDL
- Install MDL
- Apply a color theme with MDL
- Implement MDL layouts
- Create MDL cards
- Take a look at Angular.js and other frameworks

Before exploring the different design tools, we need to take a look at how designing for desktops differs from designing for mobile devices. The extra space available to us means that a different set of metrics and layouts can be utilized to make the most of this.

Desktop layouts

The enormous variety of layouts employed on the Web makes for an interesting set of challenges. A typical desktop layout for a web page has many of the features similar to those of the layouts we've covered so far, such as an app bar and side navigation drawers. Following is one such example:

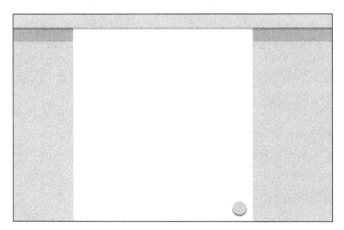

The preceding example has a primary toolbar (known as a navigation bar on desktop apps) just as its mobile counterparts do. On a desktop, this component should always be present and is 64 dp high unless it is expanded, in which case, it should be 128 dp. The navigation drawers can, and often do, have secondary toolbars of their own, as can the main content canvas as well.

Desktop navigation drawers can be fixed or opened from the navigation bar's icons. The bar has a 20 dp padding at the top and bottom, one padding of 24 dp to the right and left, and the title text is indented 80 dp from the left-hand side edge. The maximum width for the left navigation drawer is 400 dp. The right-hand side one can be variable depending on its content.

 When working with wider screens, it is often a better use of space to use tabs across the top rather than use a navigation drawer. These tabs have a minimum width of 160 dp, a maximum width of 264 dp, and a height of 48 dp.

Installing and employing web frameworks is a simple task; we simply place the framework files inside our project directory, set up a link to them in our `index.html` file, and start coding. However, keeping track of dependencies and updates, especially if we are using more than one framework, can become something of a chore. This can be largely avoided, thanks to the help from package managers, which keep our frameworks nicely up-to-date with a minimum input from us. There are a lot of such package managers around; however, very few people would disagree that Bower is by far the best suited for our needs here.

Package management

Package managers are by no means essential to install web frameworks, and depending on our needs, there are several ways to install/implement web frameworks:

- Download files directly into a project folder
- Link to the framework via a **Content Delivery Network (CDN)**
- Build the project yourself from the source code
- Install using a package management tool such as Bower

To install Bower on your system, you will first need to install the **Node Package Manager (NPM)**, which can be done from the Node.js website: `https://nodejs.org/en/`.

This is a straightforward installation, after which you can install Bower from the command window with the following:

```
npm install -g bower
```

The `-g` installs Bower globally, so it can be accessed from any of your projects. The most commonly used and most useful Bower commands are the following:

```
bower install <package>
bower update <package>
bower search <containing>
bower list
```

Using Bower update without specifying the package will update all the installed packages. If you are yet to decide which technologies you are going to adopt, you may want to install them directly or link them to a CDN before you decide. In the following examples, we will demonstrate both these techniques.

Materialize

Materialize is one of the easiest ways to implement Material Design in our web pages, as well as very helpful in automatically adjusting elements such as text size to take differing screen sizes. It provides a limited but pertinent set of material components, such as navigation drawers, ripple effects, and cards. The best way to learn about Materialize is to try it out for ourselves.

Setting up

If you have ever used Bootstrap, you will recognize immediately how Materialize is structured. You will begin by downloading the files from this link: `http://materializecss.com/getting-started.html`.

You will note that there are two main downloads available, **Materialize** and **Sass**:

Until you become familiar, and for the sake of this exercise, it is recommended to start with the standard version. From a learning point of view, downloading the files is a better option, as this allows us to examine and edit these files. However, you can also use a CDN to access these resources remotely. This has the advantage of lightening the load on our servers slightly and can often lead to quicker loading times. The HTML for the CSS components is as follows:

```
<link rel="stylesheet"
href="https://cdnjs.cloudflare.com/ajax/libs/materialize/0.97.1/css/
materialize.min.css">
```

For the JavaScript, use the following:

```
<script src="https://cdnjs.cloudflare.com/ajax/libs/
materialize/0.97.1/js/materialize.min.js">
</script>
```

The files you have downloaded simply have to be placed in your project directory alongside your `index.html` file. If you take a look around, you will see that there are two versions of the CSS and JavaScript files. The `materialize.min.css` and `materialize.min.js` files have been compressed, and these are the files you should use in your published site, as they consume less space. The uncompressed versions are far better for developing, as they are far more readable as can be seen by examining them.

With our downloaded files in the right place, linking them in HTML is very simple. The minimum code required is this:

```
<!DOCTYPE html>
<html>

<head>
<title>Materialize Demo</title>
<link type="text/css" rel="stylesheet" href="css/materialize.min.css"
media="screen,projection"/>
</head>

<body>
. . .
<script type="text/javascript"
src="https://code.jquery.com/jquery-2.1.1.min.js">
</script>
<script type="text/javascript"
src="js/materialize.min.js">
</script>
</body>

</html>
```

This, of course, will produce a blank page. To check that we have really linked our project correctly, add the following code to the top of the body tag:

```
<nav class="amber lighten-2">
<div class="nav-wrapper z-depth-1">
<div class="container">
<a href="#!" class="brand-logo">Materialize Demo</a>
</nav>
```

This will produce a navigation toolbar, as can be seen here:

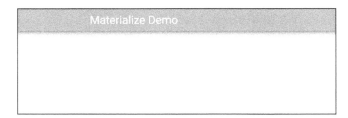

With very little coding, we have produced an app bar with the correct font, size, and spacing. We will return to the `container` class shortly as this is significant, but for now, note that shadow and elevation are generated here with z-depth. This does not give us the flexibility that Android does, and we only have five levels of elevation available, as shown in the following screenshot. This is a limitation of the framework rather than the platform itself.

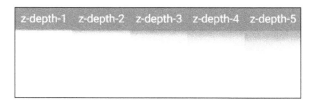

 Materialize produces very flexible UIs that adapt to the screen size of the browser they are running on. To inform browsers that the page is optimized for handheld devices, use this code: `<meta name="viewport" content="width=device-width, initial-scale=1.0"/>`.

Although the Materialize package comes with material icons and the Roboto font, many people like to include other Google icons, which can be done using the following code within the HTML head:

```
<link href="http://fonts.googleapis.com/icon?family=Material+Icons"
rel="stylesheet">
```

Material theme

We were also able to set the background color with `nav class="amber lighten-2"`. The lighten setting is not usually required in a toolbar and is just included as an example. As with z-depth, there are five settings from lighten-1 to lighten-5. There are also accent and darken settings, and between the three, we can very easily create the same color themes that we did for mobiles. We can also use hexadecimal values, as can be seen from the following image:

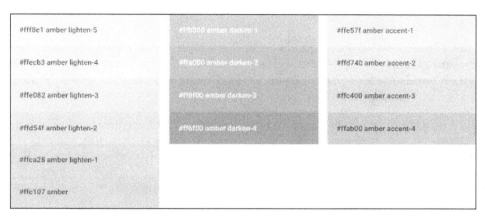

Applying our color theme to a page is only the beginning; we need to know how to lay out our pages and add some of the familiar material features and components, such as ripple effects and cards. Firstly, we need to look at the general layout of Materialize web pages and how grids with a fixed number of columns are used to create material-compliant layouts that adapt to different screen sizes.

Layouts and grids

Whatever approach we take to design an interface, be it material or any other type of design, we have to consider how this will appear on very different sizes of screens. Materialize makes use of a grid system as used in traditional graphic design to organize pages:

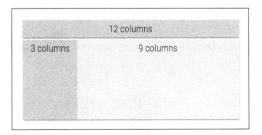

These grids are made up of 12 columns that not only allow a lot of pleasing ratios, but also provide a way to easily configure layouts for both desktop and mobile browsers. The preceding layout can be achieved with the following HTML:

```
<div class="row">
<div class="container">
<div class="col s12">12 columns</div>
<div class="col s3">3 columns</div>
<div class="col s9">9 columns</div>
</div>
```

The `container` class we mentioned earlier is a simple but a useful way of centering content and creating 15 percent margins on each side of a desktop screen and 12.5 percent on handsets. More often, it can be used when defining the whole body, but can also be placed almost anywhere.

It should be easy to see from the code how column widths are assigned. The s prefix (the `.s` class) stands for small and instructs the host browser to apply these column widths on phone screens. However, defining them for only one screen size will have the same affect on all screens, and we could just as easily use m or l for medium tablets or large desktops. Tablets are defined with any screen width between 600 and 992 px.

The example here may work fine on a desktop, but on a small screen, the three-wide column may be too narrow. This can easily be catered to with the following edit:

```
<div class="row">
<div class="container">
<div class="col s12">full width</div>
<div class="col s12 m3">full width on phones</div>
<div class="col s12 m9">full width on phones</div>
</div>
```

Alternatively, we could have simply made the column a little wider on handsets or, could have a separate setting for each format, such as the following:

```
<div class="col s5 m4 l3">variable width</div>
<div class="col s7 m8 l9">variable width</div>
```

On some occasions, there will be times when we would rather not display a component at all on a small device, in which case we can use this:

```
<div class="hide-on-small-only"></div>
```

Having seen quickly how we layout our pages, we can now see how to add content.

Cards

Cards are the most widely used material components, and this is true for desktop apps as much as any other platform. They are very simple to implement with Materialize. It is a good idea to nest the code inside a `container` class and probably within a row with `col` class definitions so that you can account for different form factors:

```
<div class="card">
<div class="card-image">
<img src="../images/autumn.jpg"/>
<span class="card-title">Postcard</span>
<div class="card-content">
<p>Having a great time.</p>
<p>Weather is lovely.</p>
<p>Wish you were here xxx</p>
</div>
<div class="card-action">
<a href="#">send</a>
<a href="#">save</a>
</div>
</div>
</div>
```

It is also possible to set the maximum height of a card with the following:

```
<div class="card small|medium|large">
```

This produces cards with maximum heights of 300, 400, and 500 dp.

 As it stands, the preceding card will not elevate when the cursor passes over it. This can be achieved with `<div class="card-panel hoverable">` and can be used on most elements and not just cards.

As ubiquitous as the card is, every app and page requires at least one clickable icon or button. These are very easy to introduce and use, as we shall see now.

Buttons and icons

Buttons, icons, and buttons with icons are very simple to use with Materialize and cover the range of buttons we have been using. The `font` directory we downloaded contains over 750 material icons, which can be used exactly like a font.

There are three main button types at our disposal here: the floating action button, the raised button, and the flat button. They can each be created and customized with as little as a single line of markup. Before we do so, we have to link our page to the icons by including the following line of code in the `<head>` tag of our HTML:

```
<link href="https://fonts.googleapis.com/icon?family=Material+Icons"
rel="stylesheet">
```

The following buttons and icons can then be added to this:

```
<!-- FLOATING ACTION BUTTONS -->
<a class="btn-floating btn-large waves-effect waves-light light-blue">
<i class="material-icons">thumb_up</i>
</a>

<a class="btn-floating btn-small waves-effect waves-light light-blue">
<i class="material-icons">thumb_up</i>
</a>

<!-- RAISED BUTTONS -->
<a class="waves-effect waves-dark btn light-blue">plain button</a>

<a class="waves-effect waves-light btn light-blue">                 <i
class="material-icons left">thumb_up</i>button with icon
```

```
</a>

<!-- FLAT BUTTON -->
<a class="waves-effect waves-amber btn-flat">flat button</a>
```

The classes and settings here allow us to create buttons that elevate when hovered over and to apply the ripple animation we encountered earlier in the book:

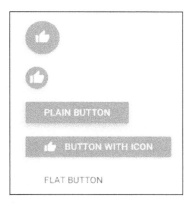

 An icon can be placed on the right-hand side of a button with the following code:

```
<i class="material-icons right">
```

The material icons that we are using here can be sized, colored, and otherwise treated like a font and can be included with the following:

```
<i class="material-icons">icon_name</i>
```

Although material icons can be sized as a font is, there is a shortcut using which we can apply size using the tiny, small, medium, and large classes. For example:

```
<i class="large material-icons">thumb_up</i>
```

A full catalog of all the 750 plus material icons can be found at the following link: `https://materialdesignicons.com/`.

A lot more could be written about Materialize, and the documentation on its site at `http://materializecss.com/` is a great place to continue. For now, we have to take a look at the other frameworks that are available, such as MDL.

Material Design Lite

The Material Design Lite framework, which is made by Google, operates in the same way as Materialize and most other CSS frameworks by providing CSS and JavaScript that are written to create material-compliant components and animations.

The Lite descriptor should not be taken to mean that MDL should be considered as being inferior or pared down. There are fewer components available to us than in many frameworks but the term Lite refers more to it being lightweight in the software sense. It has a very low memory overhead and few dependencies. Although it does have fewer components than other frameworks, it is nevertheless powerful enough to satisfy the requirements for a vast majority of material designers and developers. Furthermore, its light weight lends itself to working alongside other libraries and frameworks.

As with Materialize, MDL can be either downloaded and included in our project directories, or linked via a content delivery system. Either way, the files can be found at this link: `http://www.getmdl.io/started/index.html`.

MDL has a very handy theme preview tool on their site under the **CUSTOMIZE** tab:

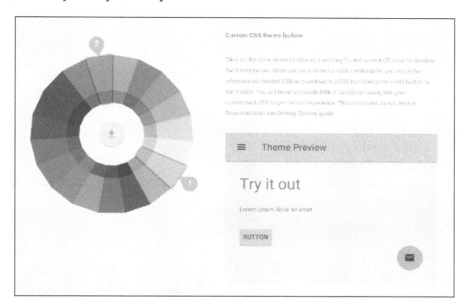

This will generate a `min.css` file, which you can either download from the center of the color wheel, replacing the one in your project folder, or edit the link in the head element of your `index.html` file to match, for example:

```
<link rel="stylesheet" href="https://storage.googleapis.com/code.
getmdl.io/1.0.5/material.amber-light_blue.min.css" />
```

With a theme in place, we can now see how the other common elements of a material web app are applied, starting as before with layouts.

Layouts and grids

MDL uses a slightly different HTML structure for its grid such that each row is contained in a nesting `div` element. The simple two-row structure that we built earlier in Materialize can be replicated in MDL with the following code:

```
<div class="mdl-grid">
<div class="mdl-cell mdl-cell--12-col">Twelve columns</div>
</div>

<div class="mdl-grid">
<div class="mdl-cell mdl-cell--3-col">Three columns</div>
<div class="mdl-cell mdl-cell--9-col">Nine columns</div>
</div>
```

There is no `container` class in MDL, and you will need to provide your own CSS, for example:

```
.mdl-grid {
padding: 0!important;
}

.mdl-cell {
padding: 24px 0;
background: #FF8F00;
text-align: center;
}
```

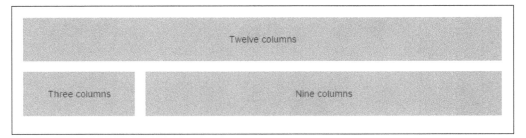

Hopefully, the similarities and differences between Materialize and MDL are becoming more apparent, and in the following section, looking at how cards are implemented in MDL will clarify things further.

Cards

MDL provides more control over components' size and shape than we saw with Materialize in the last section. As material designers, this means that we have to consider the principles we learned earlier regarding things such as font size and style, and image aspect ratios. This makes MDL flexible as well as straightforward to use.

To recreate the card from the previous example using MDL, we need to set the aspect ratio of the image section with CSS. For example:

```
.mdl-card {
width: 512px;
}

.mdl-card__title {
color: #FFF;
height: 288px;
background: url('../images/river.jpg') center / cover;
}
```

```
.mdl-card__menu {
color: #FFF;
}
```

Here, we chose the values 512 and 288 to create a 16:9 ratio. The freedom this system gives us means that we can create any ratio we like. The HTML part takes care of the rest, like this:

```
<div class=" mdl-card mdl-shadow--2dp">
<div class="mdl-card__title">
<h2 class="mdl-card__title-text">Postcard</h2>
</div>

<div class="mdl-card__supporting-text">
<p>Having a great time</p>
<p>Weather is lovely</p>
<p>Wish you were here xxx</p>
</div>

<div class="mdl-card__actions mdl-card--border">
<a class="mdl-button mdl-button--colored mdl-js-button mdl-js-ripple-
effect">Send</a>
</div>

<div class="mdl-card__menu">
<button class="mdl-button mdl-button--icon mdl-js-button mdl-js-
ripple-effect">
<i class="material-icons">share</i>
</button>
</div>
</div>
```

It is good to that see that with MDL, we can create more suitable shadows and set elevation in dp using the `mdl-shadow` class and do not have to estimate the depth as we did with Materialize. `ripple-effect` too is very simple to implement as is the card menu, which also demonstrates how icons are implemented.

The classes provided by MDL cover nearly all our design needs, and as mentioned earlier, MDL is designed to work alongside other frameworks, a feature particularly helped by the fact that all MDL classes begin with the `mdl-` prefix that avoid any clashes.

We will continue using MDL in the concluding chapters, so this will suffice as an introduction. MDL provides most of our design needs and is perfect to learn Material Design for the Web; however, it does have some limitations, and as our expertise grows, we will find ourselves wanting to explore other avenues, and there is, of course, a wide selection of tools we could use.

Alternative frameworks and libraries

There are a good number of web frameworks and libraries designed to implement Material Design and these differ in the number of components they provide and the levels to which they can be customized. Undoubtedly, the most powerful framework is **polymer**.

Polymer is a framework that uses Web Components. These are a set of standards that allow web developers to reuse and customize widgets and other components in a way similar to traditional component-based development. Polymer provides a wide range of these elements, and those that will interest us, as material designers, are the paper elements.

Polymer is a powerful and flexible tool but it also requires a fair degree of technical know-how. For example, it is not a simple matter to test your site locally, and you will need to set up a server with Python, or test on a remotely hosted server.

To install polymer using Bower, use the following:

```
bower install --save Polymer/polymer#^1.0.0
```

Paper elements are not part of the default library and have to be installed separately. The full set of polymer elements can be found at: `https://elements.polymer-project.org/?utm_source=scotch.io`.

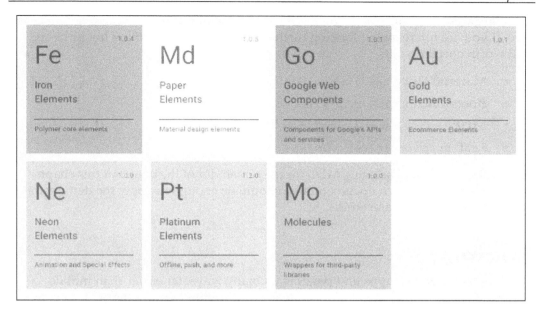

The catalog contains the full list of paper elements and these can be installed directly from the command window with `bower install polymerelements/<element>`, for example:

```
bower install polymerelements/paper-card
```

Polymer's true power lies in the way elements can be easily customized and the way data is encapsulated. As a framework, polymer takes more time than most to master, although the rewards are a far more flexible and powerful tool than the others.

Another all-purpose web framework that contains material elements is Angular JS. This well-established tool attempts to occupy the middle ground between a library of JavaScript functions and an empty but complete HTML project. The material branch of Angular is **Angular Material**, which can be found at: `https://material.angularjs.org/latest/`.

The way in which Angular is implemented is very intuitive. For example, a button may be customized simply like this:

```
.md-button {
font-size: 14px;
margin: 16px 8px 16px 8px;
min-width: 72px;
padding: 0 8px 0 8px;
text-align: center;
text-transform: uppercase;
}
```

There are a growing number of material frameworks, and they are too many to cover here. If you are interested in looking further into the topic, the following links are well worth checking out:

- **Material UI**: http://www.material-ui.com/#/home
- **Bootswatch Paper**: http://bootswatch.com/paper/#
- **MUI**: https://www.muicss.com/
- **Leaf**: http://getleaf.com/

As mentioned, we will be using MDL for the remainder of the book but this chapter and the frameworks' own documentation should be enough to apply the demonstrated points to any of these frameworks.

Summary

Building material web apps and pages is, in many ways, far easier than mobile devices. A great deal of the work is done for us. Provided we are happy to accept out-of-the-box solutions, material web UIs can be assembled in minutes. Frameworks such as MDL and Materialize are very well documented and very easy to become familiar with quickly. Many frameworks can work together, allowing us to select the features we want the most.

Spending the time to master a more sophisticated tool such as polymer is very often worth the effort, as the level of customization that the framework can provide will open up a world of possibilities.

Material design is ultimately a visual language and should transcend individual tools and platforms. It is the principles regarding proportion, light, color, and motion and not which HTML tag we use or which library we download that make an interface a material one or otherwise. Material Design websites and apps are becoming more and more abundant, and as we shall see in the next chapter, the lessons learned in the earlier part of the book can be applied equally well to desktop screens and the Web; it is simply a matter of using a different toolset.

The Materialize Framework

9

We introduced the Materialize framework in the previous chapter and set up a project with it. There is a lot more to the framework than we have seen and it contains extensive CSS and JavaScript elements, as well as many predefined material components. One of Materialize's greatest strengths is the minimal amount of code required to implement Material Design. This means that we can cover a lot of ground in this chapter, as most components and elements can be demonstrated quickly and easily, starting with the built-in material components.

It should be noted, particularly for those without a lot of experience with frameworks, that there are many more components available than those covered here. Web frameworks generally, and not just Material Design ones, make available all of the commonly found components such as buttons, checkboxes, and sliders.

In this chapter, you will learn how to:

- Create a collection list
- Add badges to list items
- Include a logo and links to a navigation bar
- Add a drop-down menu to the navigation bar
- Include text input fields
- Apply responsive text fields
- Generate wave animations
- Customize a wave animation
- Configure and apply collapsibles
- Implement tab divisions of content
- Display images with Material box

Components

Materialize comes with a good collection of material components, such as cards and buttons, which we saw in the previous chapter as well as how to set them up. As a reminder, the minimum HTML you will need in your `index.html` file is as follows:

```
<!DOCTYPE html>
<head>
<title>Materialize Demo</title>
<link type="text/css" rel="stylesheet" href="css/materialize.min.css"
media="screen,projection"/>
</head>

<body>
    . . .
<script type="text/javascript"
    src="https://code.jquery.com/jquery-2.1.1.min.js">
</script>
<script type="text/javascript"
    src="js/materialize.min.js">
</script>
</body>
```

The markup for these components is intuitive and very simple to follow and allows us to produce material-compliant interfaces in next to no time. One of the most common components on any Web page is item lists.

Lists and badges

Materialize provides the `collection` class for organizing content into lists. For example, the following HTML will produce a nicely divided list:

```
<ul class="collection">
<li class="collection-item">Jellybean</li>
<li class="collection-item">Kit-kat</li>
<li class="collection-item">Lollipop</li>
<li class="collection-item">Marshmallow</li>
</ul>
```

It is very easy to add to this setup. For example, the following edit would add a header to the list.

```
<ul class="collection with-header">
<li class="collection-header"><h4>Android versions</h4></li>
<li class="collection-item">Jellybean</li>
    ...
</ul>
```

Items can be turned into links as shown next:

```
<div class="collection">
<a href="some_link.html" class="collection-item">Jellybean</a>
...
</div>
```

These links can be highlighted with <href="some_link.
html" class="collection-item active">.

One of the most common components on material web pages is the badge. These are small notifications that are normally used to inform the user that a new or yet unseen event has occurred, such as a new or unread message from a contact. Badges come in two flavors: regular and new, as can be seen in the following screenshot:

Badges are very simple to implement, as the following code demonstrates:

```
<div class="collection">
<a class="collection-item">Adam</a>
<a class="collection-item">Betty<span class="new badge">1</span></a>
<a class="collection-item">Carl<span class="badge">3</span></a>
<a class="collection-item">Deborah</a>
</div>
```

The list items demonstrated here are very simple and contain only a single line of text, or a link, but they can be customized to suit more complex purposes using regular HTML elements, such as `<p>` and `<br>`, to add extra lines, and `<src>` to include imagery. In fact, one of Materialize's main advantages is how easy it is to include familiar HTML structures. This can be very clearly seen in other components too, such as the navigation bar.

Navigation bars, menus, and icons

We touched briefly on the navigation bar in the previous chapter, but this component generally makes up a significant part of an interface, as it generally contains top-level navigation, and requires a closer look.

Materialize allows us to easily add links, icons, and drop-down menus to our navigation bar, to align elements, and to configure them to work on a variety of screen sizes.

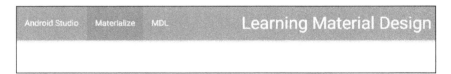

The preceding screenshot can be generated with the following markup:

```
<nav>
<div class="nav-wrapper">
<a class="brand-logo right">Learning Material Design</a>
<ul  class="left hide-on-med-and-down">
<li><a href="some_link.html">Android Studio</a></li>
<li><a href="some_link.html">Materialize</a></li>
<li><a href="some_link.html">MDL</a></li>
</ul>
</div>
</nav>
```

This code is very straightforward, and we could have had the logo on the right-hand side and the links on the left, had we omitted `right` in the third row and `left` in the fourth. The use of `hide-on-med-and-down` ensures that the links will not show up on medium or smaller screens, and Materialize is so responsive that you can demonstrate this simply by resizing your browser window. Icons can be included in the same way as we did in the last chapter.

To indicate which page the user is currently on, we can set a link to be highlighted as current with `<li class="active">Materialize</li>`, and this can be seen in the previous screenshot.

As you would imagine, implementing a drop-down menu can be achieved with very little code, but it is very slightly more involved than the previous elements.

A drop-down menu requires two elements: a definition and an activation. A definition might look something like this:

```
<ul id="my_menu" class="dropdown-content">
<li><a>menu item</a></li>
<li><a>menu item</a></li>
<li class="divider"></li>
<li><a>menu item</a></li>
</ul>
```

We can then activate this from wherever we want our menu using this markup:

```
<li><a class="dropdown-button" data-activates="my_menu">Menu<i
class="material-icons right">arrow_drop_down</i></a></li>
```

In this example, we added text and an icon simply by way of demonstration, and usually only one of these will be required. Finally, we need to add a little bit of JavaScript. This can be added anywhere in the code, providing it comes after jQuery is loaded with the following line:

```
<script src="https://code.jquery.com/jquery-2.1.1.min.js"/>
```

The function itself should look like this:

```
<script type="text/javascript">
  $(document).ready(function(){
    $('.dropdown-button').dropdown();
  });
</script>
```

Interfaces very often require some form of user input, and the way that Material Design handles text field input is characteristically intuitive and elegant, as we shall see next.

Text input and display

The Material Design approach to user text input is not only attractive, but it also manages space very efficiently, and clearly informs users as to what is happening and what is expected of them.

When a material text input field is selected by the user, the input prompt, or placeholder, slides elegantly up and away from the input area, which itself is then highlighted. This approach not only uses less space than traditional text input techniques, but is also highly intuitive.

The preceding input field can be created with markup along the lines of the following:

```
<div class="row">
<form class="col s12">
<div class="row">
<div class="input-field col s6">
<input id="place_of_birth" type="text">
<label for="place_of_birth">Place of birth</label>
</div>
</div>
</form>
</div>
```

A hint can be placed in the input area by using a `placeholder` definition as shown as follows:

```
<input placeholder="A Hint" id="place_of_birth" type="text">
```

Other `input`types include `password` and `email`, and icons can be added by including a tag, such as the following one, before the `<input>` tag:

```
<i class="material-icons prefix">phone</i>
```

Larger text fields can be produced as shown next:

```
<textarea id="my_textarea" class="materialize-textarea"></textarea>
```

Unlike many other material frameworks, Materialize not only dynamically resizes widgets and frames to suit different screen and window sizes, but can also change font size and line spacing to make lengthy text read easily on any device. This is achieved with Materialize's `flow-text` class, and it will even resize text as the user resizes a browser window. It can be implemented as shown here:

```
<p class="flow-text">Lengthy text goes here...</p>
```

Materialize provides a lot of very useful components, and is one of the most responsive frameworks available for Material Design. Of course, Material Design really comes into its own when we apply motion in the form of transitions and animations.

Transitions and motion

One of Material Design's most appealing characteristics is the way elements move. Having content slide in and out of view allows us to manage data in a way that keeps the interface as uncomplicated as possible, while allowing users to access deeper content as and when they choose.

Wave animations

The wave effect is probably the most widely recognized material animation, and implementing it with Materialize could not be easier. In its simplest form, it looks like this:

```
<a class="btn waves-effect">OK</a>
```

The default implementation provides a gray ripple effect, but the framework provides seven other colors, plus a simple way to generate our own custom colors with CSS. The seven provided colors are:

```
waves-light
waves-red
waves-yellow
waves-orange
waves-purple
waves-green
waves-teal
```

They are implemented as shown here:

```
<a class="btn waves-effect waves-purple">OK</a>
```

These colors are fine for very many purposes, but creating our own custom waves is very simple, as can been seen in the following snippet, which creates an amber wave effect.

```
.waves-effect.waves-amber .waves-ripple {
  background-color: rgba(253, 153, 0, 0.7);
}
```

It is important to set the alpha channel to 70 percent opaque so that the button text is still visible during the animation.

Waves can also be configured to create a circular pattern, rather than a rectangular one, by simply adding the `waves-circle` class, as shown here:

```
class="waves-effect waves-circle waves-teal
```

Confirming user interaction with motion is one of Material Design's stronger features. Another is to use motion to reveal and hide content according to its relevance. Materialize achieves this very nicely with a set of accordions and pop-outs called collapsibles.

Accordions and pop-outs

Frames that collapse and expand to hide and reveal information are a very useful way to organize content, as they keep the interface simple but still allow the user to access the information that interests them.

The preceding screenshot demonstrates how the accordion looks before it is clicked on, and the following one shows its state once an item has been selected:

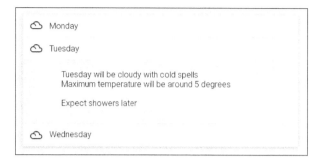

The collapsible is contained in an unordered list tag like this:

```
<ul class="collapsible" data-collapsible="accordion">
```

Each item is then contained in a `<li>` tag, as shown as follows:

```
<li>
<div class="collapsible-header"><i class="material-icons">cloud</
i>Tuesday</div>
<div class="collapsible-body"><p>Tuesday will be cloudy with cold
spells<br>Maximum temperature will be around 5 degrees<br><br>Expect
showers later</p></div>
</li>
```

Materialize collapsibles come in two flavors: the inline accordion, as seen earlier, and a pop-out version that provides a little more emphasis on the selected item, as shown next:

To apply a pop-out accordion, simply add the `popout` class like this:

```
<ul class="collapsible popout" data-collapsible="accordion">
```

Collapsibles can also be configured to open with one or more items already visible. Simply add the `active` class, as shown here:

```
<div class="collapsible-header active"><i class="material-
icons">cloud</i>Tuesday</div>
```

This way, the collapsibles we have touched on here will only open one segment at a time. However, it is quite possible to have more than one open, and this can be achieved by changing the class from `accordion` to `expandable` like this:

```
<ul class="collapsible" data-collapsible="expandable">
```

Expandables and collapsibles are not the only way to neatly organize and hide content that is not relevant. Another way is through the use of tabs, and as we will see next, Materialize provides classes to implement material-compliant tabs.

Dividing content with tabs

Tabs are not a new way to divide content, and have their origin in paper stationary. The only difference with material tabs is their appearance—in particular, the pleasing way in which the tab underscore animates as it switches from one to another, and of course, the use of the Roboto family of fonts.

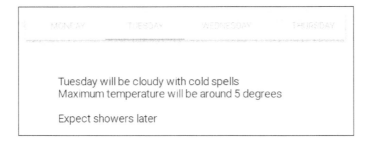

As we have come to expect, the implementation of material tabs is remarkably simple with Materialize. A structure such as the preceding one can be implemented with the following HTML:

```
<div class="row">
<div class="col s12">
<ul class="tabs">
<li class="tab col s3"><a href="#mon">Monday</a></li>
<li class="tab col s3"><a href="#tue">Tuesday</a></li>
```

```
<li class="tab col s3"><a href="#wed">Wednesday</a></li>
<li class="tab col s3"><a href="#thu">Thursday</a></li>
</ul>
</div>
<div id="mon" class="col s12">Some content</div>
<div id="tue" class="col s12">Tuesday will be cloudy with cold
spells<br>Maximum temperature will be around 5 degrees<br><br>Expect
showers later</div>
<div id="wed" class="col s12">Some content</div>
<div id="thu" class="col s12">Some content</div>
</div>
```

Just as with collapsibles, tabs can be set as open by default or as disabled and unavailable to be opened. These can be achieved with the following edits:

```
<li class="tab col s3"><a class="active" href="#mon">Monday</a></li>
<li class="tab col s3 disabled"><a href="#tue">Tuesday</a></li>
```

Material design not only provides great ways to display and organize textual content, it is also a fantastic framework to show off high-quality imagery.

Displaying images

Materialize provides a very cool lightbox-like plugin to display single images and image carousels. Material box images communicate their interactivity by lightening up as the pointer moves over them, and once clicked, the image enlarges, centers itself, and darkens the background.

Adding a single image is very simple and utilizes familiar HTML tags, for example:

```
<img class="materialboxed" data-caption="A caption" width="640"
height="426" src="images/some-image.jpg">
```

This defines the size of the image and adds an optional caption at the foot of the image. This provides a very pleasing way to showcase individual images, but Material box really comes into its own when displaying a series of images in a slider or carousel fashion. To implement a carousel, we use the slider and slides classes, which must be nested as shown:

```
<div class="slider">
<ul class="slides">
    ...
</ul>
</div>
```

The individual images are expressed as list items and can be defined as shown in the following example:

```
<li>
<img src="images/fall-leaves.jpg">
<div class="caption left-align">
<h3>A large caption</h3>
<h5 class="light grey-text text-lighten-2">With a smaller subtitle</
h5>
</div>
</li>
```

We could also have used center-align or right-align on the text, which also slides the caption into view from the appropriate direction.

Material design is very much a visual language, and presenting images elegantly lies at the very heart of most material interfaces, and Materialize implements this in an easy-to-follow fashion.

Summary

The Materialize framework provides a very good balance between power and simplicity. With a little knowledge of HTML, attractive interfaces can be put together very quickly and efficiently.

Another advantage of using a framework like this is that we don't need to overly concern ourselves with matters such as metrics and typography, because the material guidelines are applied automatically.

For the more adventurous, Materialize also provides some powerful JavaScript plugins to track and respond to users' navigation around a page, and to further customize components.

There are a growing number of user-friendly CSS frameworks for Material Design, and each has its own advantages and disadvantages. Materialize occupies a position that sits nicely between ease of use and sophistication. It is easy to pick up, and with a little effort, complex and beautiful interfaces can be designed.

Another easy-to-learn but powerful framework is **Material Design Lite** (**MDL**), which we encountered briefly in the previous chapter. We will return to MDL in the next chapter and dig a little deeper to see just what we can achieve with it.

10
Material Design Lite

In the last chapter, we saw how the Materialize framework provides an intuitive way to create material web pages. **Material Design Lite (MDL)**, as we saw in *Chapter 8, Material Web Frameworks*, offers a similarly simple mechanism and is probably even easier to pick up. The reason for this is the slightly different approach used by MDL. This approach involves starting with standard HTML elements and then adding the MDL classes. This not only makes it very easy to learn, but also makes it the ideal tool for adapting our existing web pages into Material Design ones. Perhaps the best way to think of MDL is as an enhanced set of traditional HTML components. Another differing feature is how many of the desired effects can be implemented with some very simple and intuitive CCS.

In this chapter, you will learn how to:

- Create a page layout with a transparent header
- Add navigation options
- Customize the header
- Include a side bar
- Add tabs
- Create a search field
- Add drop-down menus
- Implement forms
- Create floating text labels
- Apply pattern attributions
- Add tables

Components

Components lie at the heart of Material Design, and despite the framework's claim to provide only a limited set of components, MDL actually provides a comprehensive number of them. They have also been designed to meet all the material criteria we encountered earlier in the book, and in terms of appearance alone, MDL is probably the most attractive. The framework also provides some very elegant features such as transparent headers that are not available or easy to implement in other frameworks.

Headers

Most web designs begin with the overall layout, and in Material Design, this nearly always involves a navigation bar. If we are creating a site that utilizes a lot of vivid imagery, very pleasing results can be achieved with a transparent navigation bar. Firstly, it may be worth recapping how we link our `index.html` code with the framework, both of which will occupy the same directory:

```
<!DOCTYPE html>
<html>
<head>
<script src="https://storage.googleapis.com/code.getmdl.io/1.0.0/
material.min.js"></script>
<link rel="stylesheet" href="https://storage.googleapis.com/code.
getmdl.io/1.0.0/material.amber-blue.min.css">
<link rel="stylesheet"href="https://fonts.googleapis.com/
icon?family=Material+Icons">
</head>
<body>
     .  .  .
</body>
</html>
```

 Note that you should use the `.min` versions of the framework files for your published site, and the unzipped versions during development.

Navigation bars

MDL is even easier to operate than materialize, when implementing the navigation bar. We will need the following snippet of CSS, which can either be set inline or in a separate stylesheet:

```
<style>
  .my-layout-transparent {
    background: url('my-background.jpg') center / cover;
  }
  .my-layout-transparent .mdl-layout__header,
  .my-layout-transparent .mdl-layout__drawer-button {
    color: white;
  }
</style>
```

We can now add the following HTML to the body of our page:

```
<div class="my-layout-transparent mdl-layout mdl-js-layout">
<header class="mdl-layout__header mdl-layout__header--transparent">
<div class="mdl-layout__header-row">
<span class="mdl-layout-title">Learning Material Design</span>
<nav class="mdl-navigation">
<a class="mdl-navigation__link"href="">Android Studio</a>
<a class="mdl-navigation__link"href="">Materialize</a>
<a class="mdl-navigation__link"href="">MDL</a>
</nav>
</div>
</header>
</div>
```

It is more usual in such a layout to have the links right-aligned, and this can be achieved easily by including a spacer after the title:

```
<div class="mdl-layout-spacer"></div>
```

We could, of course, provide the same navigation via a sliding drawer if we chose, and this can be added after the header, with markup along these lines:

```
<div class="mdl-layout__drawer">
<span class="mdl-layout-title">Learning Material Design</span>
<nav class="mdl-navigation">
<a class="mdl-navigation__link"href="">Android Studio</a>
<a class="mdl-navigation__link"href="">Materialize</a>
<a class="mdl-navigation__link"href="">MDL</a>
</nav>
</div>
```

We can also set the sidebar to be fixed on wider screens with the following class:

```
<div class="mdl-layout mdl-js-layout mdl-layout—fixed-drawer">
```

To create a header that scrolls with the page rather than remaining fixed at the top, replace the relevant line of code with this one:

```
<header class="mdl-layout__header mdl-layout__header—scroll">
```

Alternatively, we can create a header that shrinks when the user scrolls down, but nevertheless remains visible at all times. This can be achieved with this line:

```
<header class="mdl-layout__header mdl-layout__header—waterfall">
```

The CSS component of this waterfall header looks like this:

```
.my-layout-waterfall .mdl-layout__header-row .mdl-navigation__
link:last-of-type  {
  padding-right: 0;
}
```

Tabs

Depending on the purpose of our page, it may often be preferable to organize content using tabs. This is equally easy to set up in MDL with the following header:

```
<header class="mdl-layout__header">
<div class="mdl-layout__header-row">
<span class="mdl-layout-title">Learning Material Design</span>
</div>
```

```
<div class="mdl-layout__tab-bar mdl-js-ripple-effect">
<a href="#scroll-tab-1" class="mdl-layout__tab is-active">Android
Studio</a>
<a href="#scroll-tab-2" class="mdl-layout__tab">Materialize</a>
<a href="#scroll-tab-3" class="mdl-layout__tab">MDL</a>
</div>
</header>
```

This will produce an output like the following one, along with ripple-effect animations:

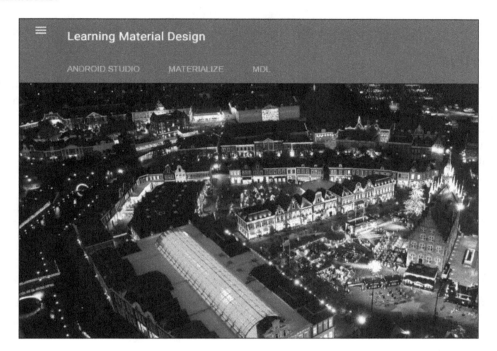

Search fields

Many material web pages, and other types as well, contain a search field in the header, and these too are simple to include. The following code demonstrates how this is done:

```
<div class="mdl-textfield mdl-js-textfield mdl-textfield--expandable">
<label class="mdl-button mdl-js-button mdl-button--icon" for="search-
expandable">
<i class="material-icons">search</i>
```

```
</label>
<div class="mdl-textfield__expandable-holder">
<input class="mdl-textfield__input" type="text" id="search-expandable"
/>
<label class="mdl-textfield__label" for="search-expandable">Search
text</label>
</div>
```

Menus

One of the most effective ways to maintain a clutter-free interface is to hide less used functions behind menus. This way, a myriad of functionality can take up no more space than a mere icon.

Menus are easily implemented and can be placed anywhere on a page, but are usually placed on the navigation bar. We can define the button that triggers the menu like this:

```
<button id="my-menu-lower-left"
   class="mdl-button mdl-js-button mdl-button--icon">
<i class="material-icons">more_vert</i>
</button>
```

With the menu itself implemented this way:

```
<ul class="mdl-menu mdl-menu--bottom-left mdl-js-menu mdl-js-ripple-
effect"
    for="my-menu-lower-left">
<li class="mdl-menu__item">New Contact</li>
<li class="mdl-menu__item">Settings</li>
<li class="mdl-menu__item">About</li>
<li class="mdl-menu__item">Close</li>
</ul>
```

For a right-aligned menu, simply use the following class instead:

```
mdl-menu—bottom-left
```

To disable a menu item and make it unavailable to the user, simply use `disabled class` rather than `class`. To add a ripple effect to a menu item, use the following line:

```
class="mdl-menu mdl-js-menu mdl-js-ripple-effect"
```

MDL menus do not strictly require CSS, but quite often a little tweaking can make a nice difference, as shown next:

```
<style>
  #my-menu-lower-right {
    margin-right: 40%;
  }

  body {
    padding: 24px;
    background: #F3F3F3;
    position: relative;
  }
</style>
```

Forms

We saw in previous chapters how the Material Design approach to entering text with floating labels is not only visually appealing, but also preserves information while using the least possible space.

Floating text labels are very simply implemented within MDL using the `<form>` HTML element and the `mdl-textfield—floating-label` MDL class.

Although there is more to it, at the simplest level, a text field with a floating label can be defined as follows:

```
<form action="#">
<div class="mdl-textfield mdl-js-textfield mdl-textfield--floating-label">
<input class="mdl-textfield__input" type="text" id="my-textfield">
<label class="mdl-textfield__label" for="my-textfield">Enter text here...</label>
</div>
</form>
```

The CSS component being as follows:

```
body {
  padding: 24px;
  background: #FBFBFB;
  position: relative;
}
```

A more traditional text field without a floating title can be produced like this:

```
<form action="#">
<div class="mdl-textfield mdl-js-textfield mdl-textfield">
<input class="mdl-textfield__input" type="text" id="my-textfield">
<label class="mdl-textfield__label" for="my-textfield">Enter text
here...</label>
</div>
</form>
```

Often, there are times when we need to be specific about the type of character being entered, such as a telephone number or zip-code. Input characters can be policed using a pattern attribute, as shown next:

```
<form action="#">
<div class="mdl-textfield mdl-js-textfield mdl-textfield--floating-
label">
<input class="mdl-textfield__input"type="text" pattern="-?[0-9]*(\.[0-
9]+)?" id="my-input-field">
<label class="mdl-textfield__label" for="sample4">Telephone
number...</label>
<span class="mdl-textfield__error">Numbers only</span>
</div>
</form>
```

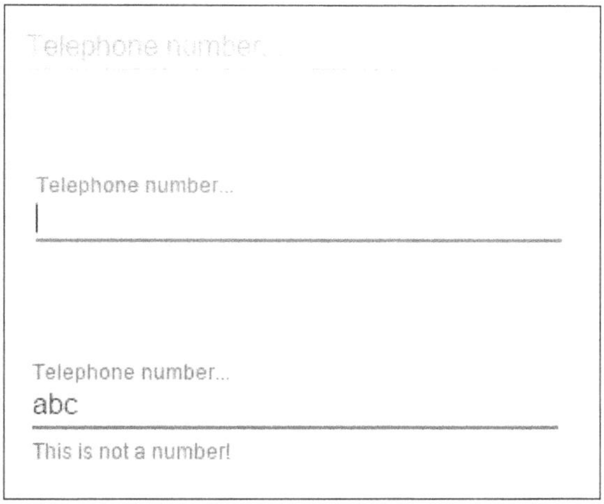

Telephone number.

Telephone number...

|

Telephone number...
abc

This is not a number!

A full list of pattern attributes can be found at:http://www.w3.org/TR/html5/ forms.html#the-pattern-attribute. When one line of input is not enough to suit our purposes, we can use the `textarea` class. For example:

```
<div>
<textarea type="text" rows="3" id="my-textarea"></textarea>
<label for="address">Your address</label>
</div>
```

There are many occasions where the data we want to express or the information we need from a user are not simply lines of text or numbers, and this is where tables come into play.

Tables

Tables of mixed content data are one of the most challenging components to present attractively, but Material Design does a fair job at this task, and in particular, the MDL version, which can apply shadows and nicely animated checkboxes.

As with other MDL components, we use traditional HTML and then include our MDL classes to provide the Material Design look and feel, as can be seen in the following markup:

```
<table class="mdl-data-table mdl-js-data-table mdl-data-table--
selectable mdl-shadow--2dp">
<thead>
<tr>
<th class="mdl-data-table__cell--non-numeric">Item</th>
<th>Weight</th>
<th>Price</th>
</tr>
</thead>
<tbody>
<tr>
<td class="mdl-data-table__cell--non-numeric">Tea (loose leaf)</td>
<td>250g</td>
<td>$3.99</td>
```

```
</tr>
<tr>
<td class="mdl-data-table__cell--non-numeric">Coffee (ground)</td>
<td>500g</td>
<td>$4.25</td>
</tr>
<tr>
<td class="mdl-data-table__cell--non-numeric">Chocolate (drinking)</td>
<td>1kg</td>
<td>$7.95</td>
</tr>
</tbody>
</table>
```

Item	Weight	Price
Tea (loose leaf)	250g	$3.99
Coffee (ground)	500g	$4.25
Chocolate (drinking)	1kg	$7.95

MDL does not offer quite the range of components that some frameworks do, but it does implement them very elegantly, and the way it fits in so nicely with vanilla HTML makes designing web interfaces very quick and easy. Another great advantage of MDL is that it comes with some very helpful and instructive template sites. These can be found at: http://www.getmdl.io/templates/index.html.

There are a growing number of CSS and JS frameworks available to the Material Designer, and of course, for the more adventurous, there is no reason to not implement it without a framework at all, using our own stylesheets and JavaScript. For most of us though, frameworks such as MDL provide the perfect balance between power and simplicity.

Summary

This concludes our look at material frameworks and Material Design as a whole. Although based largely on traditional design principles, it nevertheless introduces some very fresh elements to digital design.

Conceived originally for the smaller screens of phones and tablets to portray a wealth of information in an uncluttered fashion, Material Design can now be found on all screen sizes from smart watches to giant TV screens.

There are, of course, a lot of ways to organize content neatly and efficiently, but Material Design offers more in the form of a design language that gives our products a uniform feel across platforms, while still allowing us to customize and give our apps and pages a brand identity without breaking the overall feel of Material Design.

At the heart of Material Design lies a set of components, such as cards and floating action buttons. These behave, as the name suggests, like a form of virtual material, with physical properties such as thickness and opacity, and exist in a virtual world where they cast shadows and move as real-world objects do, accelerating and decelerating as they move.

These principles of motion and light are independent of the tools we use to apply them, but in this book we have seen which tools are available and learned enough about them to create interfaces for both mobile apps and web pages.

The Material Design guidelines are covered perfectly well within Google's own documentation, but they provide nothing on how to implement any of these concepts with code. The code in this book demonstrates how these principles can be turned into a working interface, hopefully without straying too far from the design principles themselves.

Android Studio may have appeared daunting at first, and there is a lot to it, but it is growing into an increasingly accessible and helpful tool. For anyone with a good feel for design, it will take only a little perseverance to build on what we have learned here, and create complex and valuable applications. For the more experienced coder, hopefully we will have connected the theory of Material Design to the technical know-how required to put it into practice.

A much smaller part of the book is devoted to applying Material Design to web apps and pages, and this is partly because the mobile environment is still material's natural environment. More so because material for the web requires less technical knowledge to implement, and using CSS frameworks means that we do not have to concern ourselves with margin widths and the like, as we do with mobile apps.

Whether you are building new apps and sites, or adapting existing ones, Material Design represents a significant shift in how we interact with our devices now, and how we will in the future.

Hopefully, this book is only the beginning of a long adventure. It can be nothing more than a starting point, and with a little perseverance anyone can master any and all of the tools introduced here and create sophisticated material apps and sites in no time.

Material Design is here to stay. It is a wonderfully sweet set of ideas and concepts, and it is already changing the way we expect our devices to behave. Everyone involved in writing this book hopes that it has been, and will continue to be, useful and helpful.

Index

components, MDL
  about 150
  forms 156-158
  headers 150
  menus 154, 155
  navigation bars 151, 152
  search fields 153
  tables 158, 159
  tabs 152
content
  tab divisions, implementing 144, 145
Content Delivery Network (CDN) 119
contextual menus 48-50

D

dataset
  connecting 80, 81
densities
  categories 66
density-independent pixels (dips) 23
desktop layout structure
  exploring 118, 119
dialogs
  about 46-51
  click listeners 55
  material dialog, creating 51, 52

E

elements
  hiding 93, 94
  revealing 93, 94

F

findViewById() method 33
floating text labels
  creating 156-158
forms, MDL 156-158
fragment
  about 70
  opening 70, 71

G

Genymotion 9
gravity properties 22, 23

H

HAXM 4
header, MDL
  about 150
  customizing 150

I

images
  displaying, with Material box 145, 146
  inserting 24
  scaling 24
installation, Android Studio 4, 5

J

Java code
  used, for capturing action calls 44-46
Java JDK 5

K

keylines, sliding drawers
  about 62
  ratio keylines 64-66

L

layouts
  about 18
  LinearLayouts 20-22
  managers, adding 82-85
  RelativeLayouts 19, 20
Leanback Library 104
LinearLayouts 20-22
list
  generating 76, 77
  items, adding 78-80

M

material
about 1
action icons 34, 35
AppCompat support library,
    importing 29, 30
applying, to older devices 29
properties 3
theme, applying 30, 31
toolbar, adding 31, 33
Material box
used, for displaying images 145, 146
material color palette generator
reference link 16
Material Design Lite. *See* **MDL**
material dialog
action section 53, 54
content 52
creating 51, 52
padding, around title 52
material frameworks
Angular JS 133
Bootswatch Paper, URL 134
Leaf, URL 134
Material UI, URL 134
MUI, URL 134
polymer 132
Materialize
about 117-120
buttons 126-128
cards 125, 126
components 136
file download, URL 120
grids 123, 124
icons 126-128
layouts 123, 124
setting up 120-122
theme, setting 123
transitions 141
URL 128

material theme
about 11, 12
customizing 14, 15
styles, applying 12-14
Material TV
about 104
app structure 106-108
banners 105, 106
DetailsFragment 107
guide, URL 109
recommendation cards 108, 109
MDL
about 117, 128, 149
cards 130-132
components 150
grids 129, 130
layouts 129
template sites 159
URL 128
menus
about 46, 154, 155
contextual menus 48-50
elements, URL 46
options menus 47, 48

N

navigation bar
about 151, 152
drop-down menu, adding 139
link, including 138, 139
logo, including 138, 139
navigation components, sliding drawers
configuration qualifiers 66, 67
metrics 62-64
structure 62-64
navigation drawer
activating 68-70
NavigationView 58
Node Package Manager (NPM)
URL 119

Thank you for buying
Learning Material Design

About Packt Publishing

Packt, pronounced 'packed', published its first book, *Mastering phpMyAdmin for Effective MySQL Management*, in April 2004, and subsequently continued to specialize in publishing highly focused books on specific technologies and solutions.

Our books and publications share the experiences of your fellow IT professionals in adapting and customizing today's systems, applications, and frameworks. Our solution-based books give you the knowledge and power to customize the software and technologies you're using to get the job done. Packt books are more specific and less general than the IT books you have seen in the past. Our unique business model allows us to bring you more focused information, giving you more of what you need to know, and less of what you don't.

Packt is a modern yet unique publishing company that focuses on producing quality, cutting-edge books for communities of developers, administrators, and newbies alike. For more information, please visit our website at www.packtpub.com.

About Packt Open Source

In 2010, Packt launched two new brands, Packt Open Source and Packt Enterprise, in order to continue its focus on specialization. This book is part of the Packt Open Source brand, home to books published on software built around open source licenses, and offering information to anybody from advanced developers to budding web designers. The Open Source brand also runs Packt's Open Source Royalty Scheme, by which Packt gives a royalty to each open source project about whose software a book is sold.

Writing for Packt

We welcome all inquiries from people who are interested in authoring. Book proposals should be sent to author@packtpub.com. If your book idea is still at an early stage and you would like to discuss it first before writing a formal book proposal, then please contact us; one of our commissioning editors will get in touch with you.

We're not just looking for published authors; if you have strong technical skills but no writing experience, our experienced editors can help you develop a writing career, or simply get some additional reward for your expertise.

Responsive Web Design with HTML5 and CSS3

ISBN: 978-1-84969-318-9   Paperback: 324 pages

Learn responsive design using HTML5 and CSS3 to adapt websites to any browser or screen size

1. Everything needed to code websites in HTML5 and CSS3 that are responsive to every device or screen size.

2. Learn the main new features of HTML5 and use CSS3's stunning new capabilities including animations, transitions and transformations.

3. Real world examples show how to progressively enhance a responsive design while providing fall backs for older browsers.

Creating Flat Design Websites

ISBN: 978-1-78398-004-8   Paperback: 112 pages

Design and develop your own flat design websites in HTML

1. Learn what flat design is and how you can create your own flat design projects.

2. Discover how to create flat designs without losing any functionality or ease of use.

3. Learn how to develop your HTML website using frameworks to save time.

Please check **www.PacktPub.com** for information on our titles

HTML5 and CSS3 Responsive Web Design Cookbook

ISBN: 978-1-84969-544-2   Paperback: 204 pages

Learn the secrets of developing responsive websites capable of interfacing with today's mobile Internet devices

1. Learn the fundamental elements of writing responsive website code for all stages of the development lifecycle.

2. Create the ultimate code writer's resource using logical workflow layers.

3. Full of usable code for immediate use in your website projects.

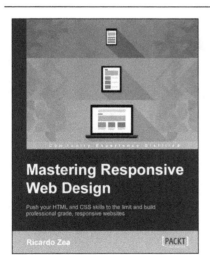

Mastering Responsive Web Design

ISBN: 978-1-78355-023-4   Paperback: 334 pages

Push your HTML and CSS skills to the limit and build professional grade, responsive websites

1. Take your RWD skills to the next level with HTML5 and CSS3 best practices that will give you a solid foundation to build out from.

2. Harness the power of the CSS pre-processor Sass to speed up the creation of your CSS.

3. Each chapter dives deep in to different aspects of RWD and is designed to get you up to speed with the latest developments in professional web design.

Please check **www.PacktPub.com** for information on our titles

www.ingramcontent.com/pod-product-compliance
Lightning Source LLC
Chambersburg PA
CBHW060133060326
40690CB00018B/3858